SPECTACULAR

NAMIBIA

ENGLISH • DEUTSCH

SPECTACULAR

NAMIBIA

TIM O'HAGAN

Photographic credits

AW=Alan Wilson; CW=Chanan Weiss; DDP=DD Photography; DSB=Daryl & Sharna Balfour; FK=Fanie Kloppers; GA=Getaway; GC=Gerald Cubitt; JdP=Jéan du Plessis; JJ=Jeremy Jowell; JK=Johan Kloppers; LPE=Leopard Photo Enterprises; MH=Martin Harvey; MS=Mark Skinner; NJD=Nigel J Dennis; PA=Photo Access; PW=Patrick Wagner; RdlH=Roger de la Harpe; RH=Rob House; SIL=Struik Image Library; VB=Vanessa Burger; WK=Walter Knirr.

Cover: JdP; **Pages 1:** JdP; **2:** GA/PW/PA; **3:** JdP; **4:** (top) JdP, (bottom) RH; **5:** (top left) JdP, (top right) WK/PA, (bottom left) DSB, (bottom right) Peter Steyn/PA; **8:** GC; **9:** (both) RH; **10:** MS; **11–13:** GC; **14–15:** DSB; **16:** NJD/DDP; **17:** JdP; **18–19:** NJD/SIL; **20–21:** JdP; **22:** MS; **23:** (top left) GA/PW/PA, (top right & bottom) JdP; **24–25:** DSB; **26:** FK/LPE; **27:** MH; **28:** RdlH/DDP; **29:** JK/LPE; **30:** JdP; **31:** JJ; **32–33:** GC; **34:** DSB; **35:** (top) DSB, (bottom) JK/LPE; **36–38:** GC; **39:** WK; **40–41:** GC; **42–43:** JdP; **44:** RdlH/DDP; **45:** VB/PA; **46:** RdlH/DDP; **47–53:** JdP; **54:** DSB; **55–57:** MH; **58–59:** AW/PA; **60:** GC; **61:** JJ; **62:** JK/LPE; **63:** Herman du Plessis; **64:** GA/PW/PA; **65:** GPL du Plessis/PA; **66:** DSB; **67:** GA/J Nel/PA; **68–69:** JdP; **70:** GC; **71:** JJ; **72:** AW/PA; **73:** JK/LPE; **74:** JdP; **75:** MH; **76–77:** CW; **78:** GC; **79:** (top) JdP, (bottom) Lex Hes; **80:** GC; **81:** JdP; **82:** RH; **83:** David Rogers; **84–85:** JdP; **86:** GC; **87:** (left) Thomas Dressler, (right) JdP; **88:** HPH/PA; **89:** LPE; **90–91:** JdP; **92:** JK/LPE; **93:** JJ; **94:** JK/LPE; **95:** (top) HPH/PA, (bottom) JdP; **96:** CW; **97:** VB/PA; **98:** JdP; **99:** Ian Michler; **100:** JdP; **101:** JJ; **102:** DSB; **103:** FK/LPE; **104:** Annette Oelofse; **105:** (all) JdP; **106:** GC; **107:** DSB; **108–110:** GC; **111:** (both) JdP; **112–114:** GC; **115–117:** GA/PW/PA; **118–119:** GC; **120:** FK/LPE; **121:** Pat de la Harpe/DDP; **122:** JdP; **123:** JK/LPE; **124–125:** GC; **126:** David Steele/PA; **127:** GA/PW/PA; **128:** MH; **129:** (top left) MH, (top right & bottom) JdP; **130:** MH; **131:** Peter Pickford/SIL; **132–134:** MH; **135:** JdP; **136–137:** GC; **138:** Rainer M Krug; **139:** JdP; **140:** Robert Müller; **141:** Anthony Bannister/Gallo Images **142–152:** GC.

FRONT COVER: Dune Elim, Sesriem; **HALF TITLE PAGE:** Petrified dune, Namib; **TITLE PAGES:** (LEFT) Dune 45, Sossusvlei, (RIGHT) Greater flamingo, Walvis Bay; **THIS PAGE:** (TOP) Himba woman, Kaokoland, (BOTTOM) Roadsign, Namib Desert; **OPPOSITE PAGE:** (TOP LEFT) Dry grass, Kalahari, (TOP RIGHT) Namib Desert, near Sesriem, (BOTTOM LEFT) Desert elephant, Huab River, (BOTTOM RIGHT) Shipwreck, Skeleton Coast.

Struik Publishers
(a division of New Holland Publishing
(South Africa) (Pty) Ltd)

Cornelis Struik House
80 McKenzie Street
Cape Town 8001
South Africa
www.struik.co.za

Garfield House
86–88 Edgware Road
LONDON W2 2EA
United Kingdom
www.newhollandpublishers.com

14 Aquatic Drive
Frenchs Forest
NSW 2086, Australia

218 Lake Road
Northcote, Auckland
New Zealand

10 9 8 7 6 5 4 3 2 1

Copyright © 2002 in published edition: Struik Publishers
Copyright © 2002 in text: Tim O'Hagan
Copyright © 2002 in map: Struik Publishers
Copyright © 2002 in photographs:
As credited on this page

Publishing manager: Annlerie van Rooyen
Design director and concept design: Janice Evans
Designer: Illana Fridkin
Managing editor: Lesley Hay-Whitton
Editor: Monique Whitaker
German translator: Friedel Herrmann
Cartographer: Steven Felmore

ISBN 1 86872 695 9

Reproduction by Hirt & Carter Cape (Pty) Ltd
Printed and bound in Hong Kong by Sing Cheong Printing Company Limited

All rights reserved. No part of this publication may be reproduced, stored in a retrieval system, or transmitted, in any form or by any means, electronic, mechanical, photocopying, recording or otherwise, without the prior written permission of the copyright owner(s) or publishers.

SPECTACULAR NAMIBIA

introduction einführung

From the scorched moonscape of the Fish River Canyon in the south, to the lush waterways of the Kunene, Kavango and Kwando rivers in the north, Namibia is an extraordinarily beautiful and varied land. With the oldest desert on earth and the treacherous Skeleton Coast, Namibia still manages to sustain an incredible variety of living things, in terrain that is as striking as it is desolate. In the south, the ashen landscape tilts gently upward from the scarred canyon of the Gariep (Orange) River to reveal vast gravel plains stretching to the horizon. To the west, the Namib Desert forms a barrier between the interior and the shores of the icy Atlantic. Further inland, petrified forests, dating back 250 million years, stand next to fossil riverbeds snaking across the dry land. Prehistoric-looking trees with gnarled branches rise up out of a boulderland of black rock, and ancient welwitschia plants, seemingly half dead, lie baking in the sun. But suddenly the landscape changes: in Sossusvlei at the southern end of the Namib-Naukluft Park, the highest dunes in the world rise up to meet the sky, their sands reflecting the ever-changing light; in the east, the gravel plains give way to yellow and gold grasslands, merging with the gentle hills of the Kalahari, the longest continuous stretch of sand in the world. In the north, the peaks of the Brandberg Mountains and other rocky islands or *Inselberge*, such as the Spitzkoppe, signpost one of the world's richest collections of rock art. Here also are the desert elephants and black rhinos of Damaraland, which, like the creatures of the Namib and Kalahari deserts, and other animals of the fossil riverbeds, have made special adaptations to survive the scorching desert conditions. In the north, Namibia's wildlife showpiece, Etosha National Park, is home to 114 mammal species, including lion, elephant, giraffe and tens of thousands of antelope. But it is the 340 species of birds, attracted by the ephemeral waters of Etosha Pan, which bring colour and vibrance to this great African game reserve, stretching 350 kilometres from east to west. And further east, beyond the Hartmann Mountains of the Kunene Region, a landscape of cone-shaped hills gives way to the palm trees and verdant waterways of the Kunene River. All this is the mystery and fascination of a spectacular land that belongs to the 21st century, but which still lies buried in the ancient sands of the past.

Von den glutheißen Mondlandschaften des Fischflußcañons im Süden bis zu den grün umsäumten Flußläufen des Kunene, Kavango und Kwando im Norden ist Namibia ein Land von außerordentlicher Schönheit und Vielfalt. Hier findet man die älteste Wüste der Welt und die Skelettküste, aber auch diese Landstriche von erschreckender Ödnis und geheimnisvoller Faszination bergen eine erstaunliche Anzahl Lebewesen. Im tiefen Süden steigt das graue Land aus den zerfurchten Schluchten des Gariep (Oranje) langsam an und breitet sich in ausgedehnten Kiesebenen aus, die bis zum Horizont reichen. Die Namibwüste bildet im Westen einen Wall zwischen dem Inland und der kalten Atlantikküste. Es gibt versteinerte Wälder, 250 Millionen Jahre alt, neben steinigen Flußläufen, die sich durch das trockene Land winden. Prähistorisch aussehende Bäume mit knorrigen Ästen ragen in einer Landschaft aus schwarzen Felsen empor. In der Sonne brüten leblos wirkende Welwitschiapflanzen aus der Urzeit. Dann verändert sich die Landschaft: Am Sossusvlei, im südlichen Teil des Namib-Naukluft-Parks, türmen sich die höchsten Dünen der Welt bis in den Himmel hinauf, ihr Sand reflektiert das ständig wechselnde Licht. Im Osten gehen die Kiesebenen in gelbliches Grasland über und verschmelzen mit den sanften Hügeln der Kalahari, der längsten ununterbrochenen Sandfläche der Welt. Im Norden sind der Brandberg und die Spitzkoppe, die zu den *Inselbergen* zählen, Wegweiser zu bedeutenden Ansammlungen von Felsmalereien. Hier leben Wüstenelefanten und Spitzmaulnashörner, die sich – wie die Lebewesen der Namib und der Kalahari – den Lebensbedingungen dieser heißen Wüstengebiete einmalig angepaßt haben. Ganz im Norden liegt die Etoschapfanne, wo 114 Säugetierarten leben, einschließlich Löwen, Elefanten, Giraffen und Tausende von Antilopen. Für Farbe und Bewegung sorgen die 340 Vogelarten, angelockt von den periodischen Gewässern der Etoschapfanne. Dieses riesige Wildreservat erstreckt sich über 350 Kilometer von Ost nach West. Noch weiter östlich, hinter den Hartmannbergen der Kuneneregion, geht die Hügellandschaft in Palmenhaine und die grün umsäumten Flußläufe des Kunene über. Mystisch und faszinierend präsentiert sich dieses Land, das zum 21. Jahrhundert gehört, aber weiterhin vom Treibsand der Urzeit bedeckt ist.

SPECTACULAR NAMIBIA

windhoek

8

CAPITAL CITY

Windhoek, the capital city of Namibia, lies in a valley encircled by the Auas Mountains to the south, the Eros and Otjihavera mountains to the east and the bush-covered Khomas-Hochland Hills to the west (ABOVE). Situated literally in the centre of Namibia, the city is unique for its extraordinary mix of modern buildings and old German architecture. The skyscrapers of its principal thoroughfare and commercial centre, Independence Avenue (OPPOSITE, TOP), rise above the city's small pavement cafés (OPPOSITE, BOTTOM). Windhoek was originally known as Ai-gams, a Nama word meaning 'firewater', a reference to the hot springs situated in the suburb of Klein Windhoek.

CITY LIFE

Windhoek, die Hauptstadt Namibias, liegt in einem Tal, umgeben im Süden von den Auasbergen und im Osten von den Eros- und Otjihaverabergen. Im Westen erstrecken sich die mit Büschen bestandenen Hügel des Khomas-Hochlandes (UMSEITIG). Die Stadt liegt genau in der Mitte von Namibia und präsentiert ein einmaliges Nebeneinander von moderner Architektur und alter, deutscher Bauweise aus der Kolonialzeit. Im Stadtkern blicken die Hochhäuser an der wichtigsten Durchgangsstraße, der Independence Avenue (RECHTS, OBEN), hinab auf kleine Straßencafés (RECHTS, UNTEN). Ursprünglich war Windhoek bekannt als Ai-gams, was in der Namasprache soviel wie ‚Feuriges Wasser' bedeutet und auf die heißen Quellen, die im heutigen Vorort Klein-Windhoek vorkommen, hinweist.

windhoek

HERERO WOMAN SELLING DOLLS

The indigenous people of Namibia are renowned for their artistic ability, and the profusion of arts and crafts on display in Windhoek is testimony to this. Woodcarvings, embroidery, carpets, paintings and leatherwork are on show at the Namibian Crafts Centre, while Independence Avenue is the city's favourite venue for open-air market stalls. Here an eye-catching selection of Herero dolls in traditional dress (ABOVE) are offered to the public, as well as displays of Owambo baskets, in all shapes and sizes (OPPOSITE). Namibians flock to the city centre for the Windhoek Street Market, which takes place in the Post Street Mall on the first and third Saturday of each month.

LOCAL BASKETWARE

Die eingeborenen Völker Namibias sind bekannt für ihr handwerkliches Geschick, und die handgefertigten Artikel, die überall in Windhoek in großer Auswahl angeboten werden, bestätigen dies. Holzschnitzereien, Stickereien, Teppiche, Malereien und Lederarbeiten werden im Namibian Crafts Centre ausgestellt. Auf der Independence Avenue bieten Straßenhändler unter anderem entzückende Puppen in der Nationaltracht der Herero an (UMSEITIG) und Owambokörbe in allen Größen und Formen (OBEN). Der Straßenmarkt, der am ersten und dritten Samstag des Monats in der Poststraßenpassage abgehalten wird, lockt viele kauflustige Namibier ins Stadtzentrum.

SPECTACULAR NAMIBIA

katatura

STREETSIDE TRADER

The township of Katatura, northwest of Windhoek, came into being in 1959 after residents of the Old Location were forcibly removed there. This occurred under South Africa's old apartheid laws, when that country still controlled Namibia. Residents of this new township aptly named it Katatura, which means 'the place we do not wish to be'. Street vendors here (ABOVE) try to make a living selling the necessities of life – clothes, shoes, food and basic furniture. While there are some luxury homes in the township, for many of the residents life is a battle for survival. Bringing some colour to the area are murals by local artists, who display their talents on the walls of homes (OPPOSITE).

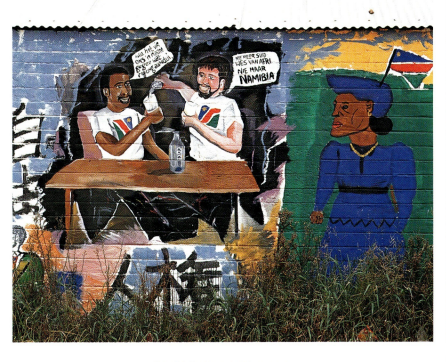

KATATURA MURALS

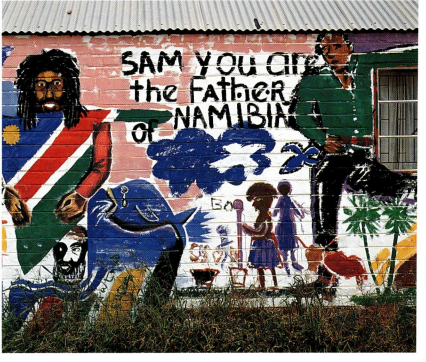

Die Wohnsiedlung Katatura, nordwestlich von Windhoek gelegen, entstand 1959, nachdem die Einwohner der ‚Alten Werft' zwangsweise dorthin umgesiedelt wurden. Zu der Zeit wurde Namibia noch von Südafrika regiert und fiel somit unter die Apartheids-Gesetzgebung. Die gegen ihren Willen Umgesiedelten nannten den Ort Katatura, das heißt ‚der Ort, wo wir nicht sein möchten'. Händler am Straßenrand (UMSEITIG) versuchen sich ihren Lebensunterhalt aus dem Verkauf von allgemeinen Gebrauchsartikeln – Kleidung, Schuhen, Nahrungsmitteln und einfachem Mobiliar – zu verdienen. Es gibt zwar auch einige Luxuswohnungen, aber die Mehrheit der Einwohner dieser Wohnsiedlung kämpft ums Überleben. Die Wandmalereien ansässiger Künstler verbreiten etwas Farbenfreude (OBEN und RECHTS).

SPECTACULAR NAMIBIA

kalahari

ENINGU CLAYHOUSE LODGE

The architecture and interiors are Mexican, but the views are distinctly African at the Eningu Clayhouse Lodge (ABOVE), 65 kilometres southeast of Windhoek International Airport. It took 80,000 sun-dried bricks made from natural clay deposits to build this lodge, and they blend perfectly with the warm, bush-covered dunes on the fringes of the Kalahari. Eningu, with its elegant swimming pool and whirlpool (OPPOSITE), won the award for Namibia's best lodge in 1997. Visitors can enjoy excellent local cuisine, game trails and the tranquillity of the Kalahari. It also boasts an archery range and volleyball and badminton courts. For the truly laid-back there are cosy hammocks slung between banana trees.

OASIS IN THE KALAHARI

Bauweise und Einrichtung sind mexikanisch, aber der Ausblick ist eindeutig afrikanisch bei der Eningu Clayhouse Lodge (UMSEITIG), die 65 Kilometer südöstlich vom Windhoeker Flughafen liegt. Es wurden 80 000 ungebrannte, sonnengetrocknete Lehmziegel aus natürlichen Lehmvorkommen benötigt, um dieses Gästehaus zu bauen. Die Steinbauten fügen sich harmonisch ein in die warme, mit Sträuchern bestandene Dünenlandschaft am Rande der Kalahari. Eningu, mit seinem eleganten Schwimmbad und Whirlpool (RECHTS), erhielt 1997 die Auszeichnung als beste Lodge Namibias. Besucher können die ausgezeichnete einheimische Küche genießen, Pirschfahrten unternehmen und die friedliche Stille der Kalahari in sich aufnehmen. Ein Schießplatz für Bogenschützen und Spielfelder für Volleyball und Federball sind auch vorhanden. Für die ganz Bequemen hat man gemütliche Hängematten zwischen den Bananenstauden gespannt.

SPECTACULAR NAMIBIA

kalahari

KALAHARI MOON RISE

The gentle, curved landscape of the Kalahari, with its ochre dunes and stretches of grassland and acacia trees, starts in southern Namibia and extends all the way into the Democratic Republic of the Congo – the longest continuous stretch of sand in the world. The beauty of the moon's ascent over the dunes (ABOVE) and of the long desert grasses is rivalled only by the colours of the cloud-swept sky (OPPOSITE). Although the Kalahari is referred to as a desert, it is more like a parkland of rich thornveld-savannah, home to a diverse population of mammals and birds. The only part of the Kalahari which truly resembles a desert is the southwestern end, which includes the fossil riverbeds of the Auob and Nossob.

SOCIABLE WEAVERS' NESTS

Die sanfte Hügellandschaft der Kalahari mit ihren ockerfarbenen Dünen und den Grasflächen und Akazienbäumen nimmt im Süden Namibias ihren Anfang und erstreckt sich bis in die Demokratische Republik des Kongo – die längste durchgehende Sandfläche der Welt. Mit dem zauberhaften Anblick des aufgehenden Mondes über den Dünen (UMSEITIG) und den hohen Halmen des Wüstengrases können nur noch die zarten Farbnuancen des leicht bewölkten Himmels konkurrieren (RECHTS). Obgleich die Kalahari immer als Wüste bezeichnet wird, ist sie vielmehr ein Wildpark mit Dornsavanne und beheimatet eine vielfältige Population von Säugetieren und Vögeln. Der einzige Teil der Kalahari, der wirklich Wüstencharakter hat, ist das südwestliche Ende, zu dem die versteinerten Flußläufe des Auob und Nossob zählen.

KALAHARI LIONESS ON THE HUNT

The southern Kalahari has been the hunting ground of large predators such as lion (ABOVE), hyaena and wild dog for hundreds of thousands of years. The Kalahari sands are also home to a variety of reptiles, including puff-adders (OPPOSITE, TOP), and the rarely-seen pangolin (OPPOSITE, BOTTOM), which have had to adapt to the seasonal availability of water in order to survive. Kalahari lions kill, on average, 47 animals a year, more than half of whom are small mammals. Although pangolins form part of their diet, lions often come off second best when they try to attack one. The pangolin curls into a tight, defensive ball, exposing its sharp, plate-like scales, which can inflict serious wounds.

DESERT ANIMALS

Die südliche Kalahari ist seit Jahrtausenden das Jagdgebiet großer Raubtiere, wie Löwen (UMSEITIG), Hyänen und Hyänenhunde. Im Sand der Kalahari lebt auch eine Vielzahl an Reptilien, einschließlich der Puffotter (RECHTS, OBEN), und das seltene Schuppentier (RECHTS UNTEN). Alle mußten sich der unregelmäßigen Wasserversorgung anpassen. Im Schnitt schlagen die Löwen der Kalahari 47 Tiere im Jahr, mehr als die Hälfte davon sind kleinere Säugetiere. Schuppentiere gehören zwar auch zu ihrer Nahrung, aber beim Angriff wird der Löwe oft verletzt, da das Tier sich fest zusammenrollt und die scharfen Schuppen gefährliche Wunden reißen können.

SPECTACULAR NAMIBIA

kalahari

SEWEJAARTJIES IN BLOOM

Sudden downpours bring a flush of colour to the Kalahari as a beautiful array of plants bursts into bloom. But these bright colours often belie the poisonous nature of some of the desert plants. The multicoloured *sewejaartjie* or everlasting (ABOVE) contains a poison that can damage the nervous system of mammals and cause permanent blindness. Another poisonous plant is the milk bush, whose flowers are encircled by a wreath of spiky thorns (OPPOSITE). The flora of the Kalahari has developed some amazing strategies for survival. Certain fruits, such as the devil's claw, grow long hooks behind their flowers, which protect them from the predations of animals.

spectacular namibia

POISONOUS MILK BUSH

Nach einem Platzregen blühen in der Kalahari oft viele verschiedene Pflanzen. Die schönen Farben täuschen allerdings auch über die Giftigkeit einiger Wüstenpflanzen hinweg. Die vielfarbigen Strohblumen oder Immortellen (UMSEITIG) enthalten ein Nervengift, das bei Säugetieren anhaltende Blindheit verursachen kann. Eine weitere Giftpflanze ist der Milchbusch, dessen Blüten durch Dornenkränze eingerahmt sind (OBEN). Die Flora der Kalahari hat verblüffende Überlebungsstrategien entwickelt. Bei gewissen Früchten, wie etwa der Teufelskralle, wachsen hinter den Blüten lange Haken, die sie davor bewahren, von Tieren abgefressen zu werden.

SPECTACULAR NAMIBIA

keetmanshoop & surrounds

22

KEETMANSHOOP QUIVER TREE FOREST

The gnarled branches and trunks of prehistoric-looking trees stand over a landscape of dolerite rocks in the Quiver Tree Forest near Keetmanshoop (ABOVE). These trees, known in Afrikaans as *kokerbome*, are named quiver trees because their fibrous, spongy branches were used to make quivers for the poisoned arrows of the San. The quiver tree and its cousin, the mopane aloe (OPPOSITE, TOP RIGHT), cope with the long seasons of drought in the Kalahari by storing water in their trunks and branches (OPPOSITE). The San knew this and cut the bark into squares to use as roofs for their makeshift dwellings in the heat of summer. When it rained the bark would absorb the water and retain it – keeping their homes cool.

DESERT ALOES

Knorrigen Stämmen und Ästen vorsintflutlich anmutender Bäume inmitten einer Landschaft von Doleritgestein sieht man sich im Köcherbaumwald bei Keetmanshoop gegenüber (UMSEITIG). Aus den Ästen fertigten sich die San Köcher für ihre Giftpfeile an. Diese Köcherbäume und ihre Verwandten, die Mopane-Aloen (OBEN, RECHTS) überstehen die langen Dürrezeiten in der Kalahari, indem sie in ihren Stämmen und Ästen Wasser speichern (RECHTS). Das wußten die San und schnitten sich Stücke aus Borke (OBEN) zurecht, um damit im heißen Sommer eine Bedachung für ihre Behelfsbehausungen zu verfertigen. Wenn es regnete, saugte sich dann die Borke voll Wasser und speicherte es und hielt dadurch die Wohnstätte kühl.

SPRING IN SOUTHERN NAMIBIA

East of Keetmanshoop, in the transition zone between the gravel plains of southern Namibia and the dunelands of the Kalahari, quiver trees adorn a countryside coloured, in spring, by a profusion of *dubbeltjies* or devil's thorn blooms (ABOVE). The Quiver Tree Forest and the surrounding countryside is typified by islands of scattered rock, whose shrubs and grasses manage to sustain wandering herds of sheep and goats in spite of the region's aridity (OPPOSITE). Some of these rocky islands consist of black dolerite known as *ysterklip* (iron rock), created 180 million years ago by the intrusion of molten lava into the Karoo sediments, and worn down over the millennia by wind and water.

HERD OF WANDERING GOATS

Östlich von Keetmanshoop, in der Übergangszone zwischen den Kiesebenen Süd-Namibias und den Dünen der Kalahari, zieren Köcherbäume eine Landschaft, die im Frühjahr von Morgensternblüten (UMSEITIG) übersät ist. Typisch für dieses Gebiet sind verstreute Gesteinsgruppen, umgeben von Gras und Sträuchern, von denen sich umherwandernde Ziegen- und Schafherden trotz Trockenheit ernähren können (OBEN). Einige dieser Gesteinsgruppen bestehen aus schwarzem Dolerit, bekannt als *Ysterklip* (Eisenfels), der vor 180 Millionen Jahren durch Eindringen flüssiger Lava in die Karoo-Sedimente entstand und über Jahrmillionen hinweg von Wind und Wasser abgetragen wurde.

SPECTACULAR NAMIBIA

fish river canyon

26

KOUTEIGN KOORU

KLIPSPRINGER ABOVE THE FISH RIVER CANYON

The great Fish River Canyon (OPPOSITE and ABOVE) cuts a rugged path through southern Namibia, revealing ramparts of eroded sandstone and a landscape unlike any other in the world. The ancient San called it *Kouteign Kooru*, after a mythical serpent which was said to have burrowed into the earth's crust to escape the hunters pursuing it. The canyon is 500 metres deep, extends 160 kilometres and is 27 kilometres wide in places.

Der große Fischflußcañon (UMSEITIG und OBEN) gräbt sich durch den Süden Namibias. Dabei kommen erodierte Sandsteinwälle und eine einmalige Landschaft zum Vorschein. Die San der Urzeit nannten ihn *Kouteign Kooru*, nach einer mythologischen Schlange, die sich unter der Erdkruste eingrub, um den Jägern zu entkommen. Der Cañon zieht sich über 160 Kilometer, ist 500 Meter tief und teilweise 27 Kilometer breit.

SPECTACULAR NAMIBIA

AI-AIS RESORT

A 19th century Nama herdsman who discovered hot springs at the southern end of the Fish River Canyon described them as Ai-Ais – 'very hot'. The name stuck, and during World War I the Germans established it as a spa and recuperation centre for wounded soldiers. Today Ai-Ais (ABOVE) is one of southern Africa's most popular spas, its mineral waters said to relieve all sorts of ailments, from arthritis to bronchitis. The small resort also serves as an ideal base for people setting out on the five-day Fish River Canyon Trail (OPPOSITE) and its springs are the perfect salve for weary limbs after the hike. The canyon, whose bedrock was laid 1,800 million years ago, is the second largest on earth.

HIKING THE FISH RIVER CANYON

Ein Namahirte entdeckte im 19. Jahrhundert eine Quelle am südlichen Ende des Fischflußcañons und beschrieb sie als Ai-Ais – ‚sehr heiß'. Der Name blieb. Im Ersten Weltkrieg legten die Deutschen dort einen Kur- und Genesungsort für verwundete Soldaten an. Heute ist Ai-Ais (UMSEITIG) eine beliebte Kuranlage; dem mineralhaltigen Wasser wird eine wohltuende Wirkung bei allen möglichen Leiden, von Arthritis bis Bronchitis, zugeschrieben. Der kleine Erholungsort dient auch als Stützpunkt für die fünftägige Wanderung durch den Fischflußcañon (OBEN), und das Quellwasser ist eine Wohltat für müde Gliedmaßen. Der Cañon nahm seinen Ursprung vor 1 800 Millionen Jahren und ist der zweitgrößte der Welt.

SPECTACULAR NAMIBIA

gariep river

THE GARIEP RIVER ON THE NAMIBIAN BORDER

Banks of rich alluvial soil, nurtured by the waters of the Gariep River (ABOVE), sustain a lush corridor of vineyards (OPPOSITE), orchards and other lucrative farming operations on the border between South Africa and the bone-dry gravel plains of southern Namibia. Until recently, this river was called the Orange, but is now known by its original Khoikhoi name, *Gariep* or *!Garib*. The river, regarded by the first African settlers as the mightiest in the world, travels 2,000 kilometres through the subcontinent, from its source in the Lesotho highlands to the Atlantic Ocean at Alexander Bay. During heavy rains, the river can be transformed from a trickle into a raging mass of water seven kilometres wide in places.

spectacular namibia

RIVERBANK VINEYARDS

Uferbänke mit fruchtbarem Schwemmboden, genährt durch den Fluß Gariep (UMSEITIG), ermöglichen einen grünen Korridor mit Weinstöcken (OBEN) und Obsthainen an der Grenze zwischen Südafrika und den staubtrockenen Kiesebenen von Südnamibia. Früher war der Fluß als Oranje bekannt, aber jetzt ist man auf den ursprünglichen Khoikhoi-Namen, *Gariep*, zurückgegangen. Dieser Fluß fließt 2 000 Kilometer durch den Subkontinent. Er entspringt im Hochland von Lesotho und endet im Atlantik bei Alexander Bay. Bei starkem Regen kann sich der Fluß von einem Rinnsal in eine reißende Wasserflut verwandeln, die stellenweise bis zu sieben Kilometer breit ist.

oranjemund

THE GARIEP'S COASTAL FLOODPLAIN

ORANJEMUND

The Gariep forms a beautiful floodplain of sandy islands and riverbanks, incised by tributaries (OPPOSITE), before it enters the Atlantic Ocean, between Alexander Bay on the South African side and Oranjemund (ABOVE) on the Namibian side. Oranjemund, one of the world's principal diamond-producing centres, was created in 1936 to house workers in the diamond areas. It is not open to the public without permission.

Der Gariep bildet eine malerische Schwemmebene mit Sandinseln und Flußufern, durchtrennt von Nebenarmen (UMSEITIG), ehe er zwischen Alexander Bay und Oranjemund (OBEN) in den Atlantik mündet. Oranjemund, eines der wichtigsten Zentren der Diamantgewinnung, wurde 1936 als Wohnsiedlung für die Arbeiter auf den Diamantfeldern gegründet. Ohne Sondergenehmigung gibt es keinen Zutritt für die Öffentlichkeit.

diamond area

SPERRGEBIET

A wilderness of wind-blown sand and rocky mountains stretches northwards from Oranjemund to Lüderitz. This is the *Sperrgebiet*, or forbidden area (ABOVE), which sparked a worldwide diamond rush after 1908 when an abundance of these valuable stones was discovered in the sand. Fortunes were made and lost, some prospectors became instant millionaires and diamond-mining towns such as Kolmanskop, Elizabeth Bay and Bogenfels sprang up overnight. Remnants of the early mines, such as this one near Oranjemund (OPPOSITE, TOP), can still be seen today. Visits to the *Sperrgebiet* (OPPOSITE, BOTTOM) are only allowed under strict supervision.

FORBIDDEN AREA

Eine windige Sand- und Felsöde erstreckt sich nordwärts von Oranjemund bis Lüderitz. Dies ist das Sperrgebiet (UMSEITIG), wo 1908 ein weltweites Diamantenfieber ausgelöst wurde, als eine große Anzahl dieser wertvollen ‚Steinchen' im Sande gefunden wurde. Manche machten das Große Geld, andere verloren es wieder. Einige Schürfer wurde über Nacht zu Millionären, und Minendörfer, wie Kolmanskop, Elisabethbucht und Bogenfels schossen aus dem Boden. Überreste der alten Minen, wie etwa diese bei Oranjemund (RECHTS, OBEN) sind heute noch sichtbar. Besuche im Sperrgebiet (RECHTS, UNTEN) sind nur unter strenger Aufsicht gestattet.

spectacular namibia

PLUMPUDDING ISLAND

The coastline of the *Sperrgebiet* (OPPOSITE) has claimed its share of casualties since diamonds were discovered here. Scores of boats, from trawlers to passenger liners, have been wrecked because of submerged reefs, heavy fog and treacherous currents. Tiny islands, such as Plumpudding Island (ABOVE), which lies near Sinclair's Island, halfway between Oranjemund and Lüderitz, have also caused their share of wrecks. Two recovery barges, working the submarine gravels for diamonds, were wrecked in stormy seas around Plumpudding Island 40 years ago. It is one of three dozen small islands used to harvest guano from the huge populations of seabirds which frequent the Namibian coastline.

SPERRGEBIET COAST

Die Küste des Sperrgebiets (OBEN) hat seit der Entdeckung der ersten Diamanten eine große Anzahl Schiffsunglücke erlebt. Viele Schiffe, ob Hochseekutter oder Passagierdampfer, fielen den versteckten Riffen, dem dichten Nebel und den trügerischen Strömungen zum Opfer. Auch winzige Inseln, wie die Plumpudding-Insel (UMSEITIG) – etwa auf halbem Wege zwischen Oranjemund und Lüderitz – verursachten Unglücke. Zwei Bagger, die auf dem Meeresboden nach Diamanten schürften, sind vor 40 Jahren dort untergegangen. Es ist eine von etwa drei Dutzend solcher kleinen Inseln, auf denen früher Guano abgetragen wurde, der von den vielen Seevögeln vor der namibischen Küste herrührt.

SPECTACULAR NAMIBIA

kolmanskop

38

KOLMANSKOP GHOST TOWN

ABANDONED IN THE NAMIB DESERT

In 1908, while sweeping sand off a track, a labourer discovered a diamond on the property of his employer, a German ganger named August Stauch. The discovery caused a sensation, and within a matter of months a mine and a small village sprang up on the slopes of Kolmanskop. The town thrived until 1950 when the miners moved south to Oranjemund, leaving the houses to the mercy of the desert (OPPOSITE and ABOVE).

Im Jahre 1908 entdeckte ein Arbeiter des deutschen Streckenwärters August Stauch einen Diamanten. Diese Entdeckung war eine Sensation, und innerhalb weniger Monate entstand eine Mine und eine Wohnsiedlung an den Hängen der Kolmanskuppe. Die Ortschaft florierte bis 1950, als die Minenarbeiter südwärts nach Oranjemund zogen und die Häuser der Wüste preisgegeben (UMSEITIG und OBEN) wurden.

SPECTACULAR NAMIBIA

kolmanskop

GHOST HOUSES

Just over half a century ago families lived, played and loved within the walls of these houses at Kolmanskop (ABOVE and OPPOSITE). Now a haunting beauty and loneliness are all that remain of a town which was once the centre of the diamond-mining industry on the southern Namibian coast. Not even the solid, Renaissance-style architecture of the double-storey mine-managers' houses has been able to withstand the Namib Desert. With the help of the wind, its sands have mounted stairways, ripped the roofs off houses, broken windows and knocked down doors. Sandstorms have even stripped the paint off the walls. Today all that remains of life in Kolmanskop is a museum and a restaurant.

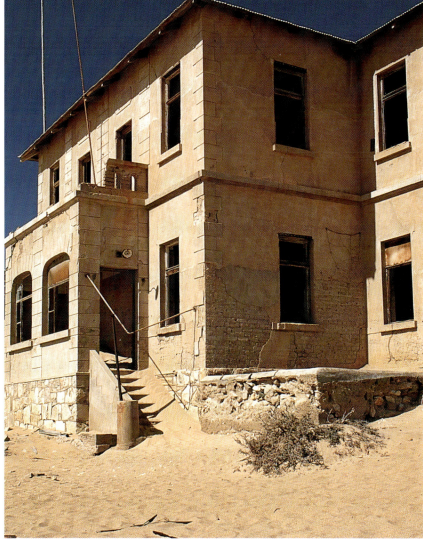

DESERTED DIAMOND-RUSH HOMES

Nur ein halbes Jahrhundert ist vergangen, seit Familien diese Häuser in Kolmanskop (UMSEITIG und OBEN) mit Leben erfüllten. Schwermütige Einsamkeit lastet über der Ortschaft, einst Mittelpunkt der Diamantengewinnung an Namibias Südküste. Nicht einmal das solide gebaute, doppelstöckige Haus im Renaissancestil, das dem Minendirektor gehörte, konnte sich gegen die Namibwüste behaupten. Mit Unterstützung des Windes gelangte der Sand über die Treppen; die Dächer wurden abgedeckt und Fenster und Türen eingeschlagen. Sogar die Farbe an den Wänden wurde durch die Sandstürme abgefräst. Nur das Museum und ein Restaurant in Kolmanskop sind noch von Leben erfüllt.

SPECTACULAR NAMIBIA

kolmanskop

42

ENCROACHING SANDS

The sun streams through broken rafters into a double-storey house at Kolmanskop, exposing a sea of sand (ABOVE). There is so much of it it looks as if the house was built into a sand dune. In the lounge the sand covers the entire floor, rising up to block half the doorway into the front room. The windows have long been broken, the doors flattened, the walls cracked. Strewn around the house are poignant mementoes of human habitation – an old shoe and a vanity case filled with sand (OPPOSITE). Outside, other deserted houses stand in the wind, ghostly beacons of an earlier age, when prospectors scrabbled in the earth for diamonds.

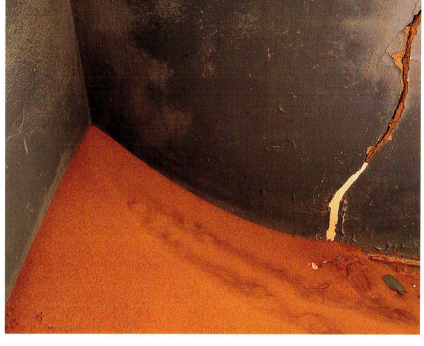

KOLMANSKOP MEMENTOES

Sonnenlicht filtert durch den zerstörten Dachstuhl eines doppelstöckigen Hauses in Kolmanskop und beleuchtet das Sandmeer (UMSEITIG). Es hat den Anschein, als ob das Haus mitten in einer Sanddüne gebaut wurde. Im Wohnzimmer bedeckt der Sand den ganzen Fußboden und füllt den Türrahmen bis zur halben Höhe. Die Fenster sind schon lange zerbrochen, die Türen aus den Angeln gedrückt und die Wände geborsten. Im Haus liegen rührende Andenken menschlicher Gegenwart umher – ein alter Schuh (RECHTS), ein Schmuckkästchen mit Sand gefüllt (OBEN). Ringsum stehen andere verlassene Häuser im Wind, gespenstische Überbleibsel einer vergangenen Zeit, als die Schürfer im Sand nach Diamanten wühlten.

SPECTACULAR NAMIBIA

lüderitz

NAMIBIA'S FIRST GERMAN SETTLEMENT

Lying between the desert and the icy Atlantic, Lüderitz (ABOVE) is a beautiful German colonial port which enjoyed sudden prosperity after diamonds were discovered at Kolmanskop. After the diamond hunters left for Oranjemund, Lüderitz went back to its old role as a fishing port and historic haven for tourists. The first German settlement in Namibia, it is built around one of the best natural harbours on the coastline, but the shallow, rocky seabed has prevented its use by ships larger than trawlers (OPPOSITE). Lüderitz got its name from Bremen tobacco merchant Adolf Lüderitz, whose emissary bought this area, then known as Angra Pequena, from a local Nama chief.

TRAWLERS, LÜDERITZ HARBOUR

Eingegrenzt zwischen Wüste und eiskaltem Atlantik, ist Lüderitz (UMSEITIG) dennoch eine hübsche Hafenstadt aus der deutschen Kolonialzeit, die nach der Entdeckung von Diamanten einen kurzen Aufschwung erlebte. Diese erste deutsche Besiedlung in Namibia ist um eine der besten natürlichen Buchten an der Westküste angelegt, aber der felsige Untergrund und mangelnder Tiefgang verhindern die Nutzung durch größere Schiffe; jetzt legen fast nur Fischkutter dort an (OBEN). Lüderitz (ehemals Lüderitzbucht) erhielt seinen Namen von dem Bremer Tabakhändler, Adolf Lüderitz, dessen Abgesandter dieses Gebiet, bekannt als Angra Pequena, von einem ansässigen Namahäuptling kaufte.

SPECTACULAR NAMIBIA

lüderitz

GERMAN COLONIAL ARCHITECTURE

The German colonial style of the houses in Lüderitz (ABOVE and OPPOSITE) is quite enchanting. The town's historical buildings make it one of the most picturesque coastal destinations in southern Africa and, because these beautifully restored homes lie at the edge of an African desert, their European character is particularly striking. Belltowers, gables and imposing double-storey homes with asymmetrical façades date back to the beginning of the 20th century, when German entrepreneurs, keen to share in the sudden wealth of the diamond fields to the south, spared no expense on their lavish homes.

ARCHITECTURAL DETAILS

Der Stil der deutschen Kolonialzeit in Lüderitz zeigt sich in den bezaubernden Häusern der Stadt (UMSEITIG und OBEN). Die historischen Bauten machen es zu einem äußerst malerischen Küstenort. Da diese schön restaurierten Häuser am Rande einer afrikanischen Wüste liegen, fällt ihre europäische Bauweise besonders ins Auge. Glockentürme, Giebel im Renaissancestil und imposante, doppelstöckige Gebäude mit asymmetrischen Fassaden gestatten einen Rückblick zum Anfang des zwanzigsten Jahrhunderts, als deutsche Unternehmer, die an dem unerwarteten Reichtum durch die Diamantenfelder im Süden teilhatten, beim Bau ihrer großzügigen Wohnhäuser keine Unkosten scheuten.

SPECTACULAR NAMIBIA

lüderitz

48

FELSENKIRCHE

Backdropped by a cloud-streaked sky above the Diamantberg is one of Lüderitz's oldest buildings (ABOVE), the *Felsenkirche* or Evangelical Lutheran Church, adjoined on the left by the pastor's residence. This church reflects one of the old architectural styles evident in the small desert town, although its southern German appearance is a departure from the typical colonial style apparent in the town's German houses. The cornerstone was laid in 1911 and the church consecrated a year later. Other attractions for visitors to Lüderitz are the jetty at the harbour (OPPOSITE, TOP) and Bogenfels Arch, the 55-metre-high outcrop of rock 90 kilometres south of the town (OPPOSITE, BOTTOM).

JETTY AND BOGENFELS ARCH

Wolkenfetzen am Himmel über dem Diamantberg bilden den Hintergrund zu einem der ältesten Gebäude in Lüderitz, der Felsenkirche (UMSEITIG). Daneben steht das evangelische Pfarrhaus. Die Kirche ist typisch für die alte deutsche Architektur, die man in diesem kleinen Wüstenort antrifft, aber das süddeutsche Erscheinungsbild ist nicht so verbreitet wie der typische Kolonialstil der deutschen Stadthäuser. Der Grundstein wurde 1911 gelegt und ein Jahr später ist die Kirche geweiht worden. Weitere Attraktionen für Besucher sind die alte Landungsbrücke am Hafen (RECHTS, OBEN) und der Bogenfels, ein 55 Meter hoher Felsbogen, der 90 Kilometer südlich der Stadt steht (RECHTS, UNTEN).

SPECTACULAR NAMIBIA

namib desert

NAMIB DUNE GRASS

Like islands of life in the dry sands of the Namib, tufts of grass spring from the base of dunes south of Lüderitz (LEFT and OPPOSITE), providing shade and food for a variety of tiny insects. *Stipagrostis sabulicola* (LEFT), a common grass which grows at the base of the shifting dunes, absorbs water from the fog which rolls in over the Atlantic, serving as a valuable source of moisture for insects such as the desert beetle. Like the taller, spikier Kalahari coach grass or *duineriet*, this grass sends out roots, stabilising the sand around it, and creating an environment for the settlement of new grasses. Apart from their nutritional value, these grasses also serve as places of refuge for small animals hiding from predators such as black-backed jackals and hyaenas.

DUINERIET

Wie Inseln auf dem Dünenmeer der Namib sprießen Grasbüschel aus dem Sand (UMSEITIG und OBEN) und bieten einer Vielzahl von winzigen Insekten Schatten und Nahrung. *Stipagrostis sabulicola* (UMSEITIG) ist eine verbreitete Grasart am Fuße der Dünen südlich von Lüderitz. Nebelschwaden, die vom Atlantik herüberwallen, versorgen das Gras und einige Insektenarten, wie die Wüstenkäfer, mit Feuchtigkeit. Gleich dem höher wachsenden, harten Dünenreet, bildet auch dieses Gras Ableger, die den Sandboden ringsum festigen und dadurch neuen Wuchs begünstigen. Diese Gräser bieten auch eine Zufluchtsstätte für kleine Tiere, die sich vor Raubtieren wie Schakal und Hyäne verstecken.

SPECTACULAR NAMIBIA

SOUTHERN NAMIB

THE WORLD'S OLDEST DESERT

Distant petrified dunes form a rugged backdrop to the sparsely grassed land of the southern Namib (OPPOSITE and ABOVE), whose sands were blown here over 80 million years ago. Although the Namib is the world's oldest desert, it is relatively young in terms of the geological evolution of Namibia, whose oldest rocks date back 1,800 million years. In spite of its apparent desolation the Namib is home to millions of tiny creatures.

Versteinerte Dünen bilden eine zerklüftete Kulisse für die spärliche Grasnarbe der Süd-Namib (UMSEITIG und OBEN), deren Sand vor 80 Millionen Jahren hierher geweht wurde. Die Namib ist zwar die älteste Wüste der Welt, aber im Hinblick auf die geologische Evolution Namibias ist sie relativ jung, denn das älteste Felsgestein datiert 1 800 Millionen Jahre zurück. Trotz scheinbarer Öde leben hier Millionen kleiner Lebewesen.

SPECTACULAR NAMIBIA

namib desert

54

DESERT ELEPHANTS

Ancient rivers, such as the Huab, Hoanib and Hoarusib, have worn deep, often fertile, valleys through the Namib. These riverbeds, known as linear oases because of their subterranean water, provide sustenance for several large mammal species, among them desert elephants (ABOVE). The Namib elephants are one of only two known populations of desert elephant in the world, the other being in Mali. Uniquely adapted to the arid, sandy conditions, they have smaller bodies and larger feet than other elephants and will walk hundreds of kilometres along dry riverbeds in search of water. Dozens of species of bird, including ostriches (OPPOSITE), also manage to survive the heat and months without rain.

NAMIB OSTRICHES

Uralte Flußläufe, wie der Huab, der Hoanib und der Hoarusib, haben tiefe, oft fruchtbare Täler in der Namib geschaffen, die dank des unterirdischen Wassers lineare Oasen sind und verschiedenen Großsäugern das Überleben ermöglichen. Dazu zählen auch die Wüstenelefanten (UMSEITIG), eine von nur zwei bekannten Populationen der Welt; die andere ist in Mali. Einzigartig dem trockenen, sandigen Umfeld angepaßt, mit kleineren Körpern und größeren Füßen als andere Elefanten, laufen sie hunderte von Kilometern in trockenen Flußläufen auf der Suche nach Wasser. Auch Dutzende von Vogelarten, einschließlich Straußen (OBEN), überleben trotz Hitze monatelang ohne Regen.

SPECTACULAR NAMIBIA

namib desert

56

DESERT TRACKS

The tiny creatures of the desert leave their own tattoos and strange geometric patterns on the scorching sands (ABOVE). Seldom seen during the heat of the day, they emerge at night, either to seek the life-giving moisture of the fog rolling in from the Atlantic, or to snatch a quick meal. Hunters (OPPOSITE) include the sand-burrowing scorpion, who lies in wait for its prey during the night, while daytime sees predators such as the horned adder and the shovel-snouted lizard on the prowl. This lizard protects its feet in unbearably high temperatures by doing an amusing little thermal dance, lifting its feet alternately off the burning sands.

CREATURES OF THE NAMIB

Die winzigen Geschöpfe der Wüste hinterlassen ihre eigenartigen geometrischen Muster im heißen Sand (UMSEITIG). Tagsüber, in der großen Hitze, sind sie selten zu sehen, aber nachts kommen sie hervor, entweder, um die lebenspendende Feuchtigkeit der vom Atlantik herüber ziehenden Nebelschwaden aufzunehmen, oder um schnell eine Mahlzeit zu erhaschen. Zu den Jägern (OBEN und RECHTS) zählt sowohl der Skorpion, der nachts seiner Beute auflauert, als auch die Hornviper und die Wüsteneidechse, die tagsüber auf Beutezug gehen. Wenn die Temperaturen unerträglich werden, schützt diese Eidechse ihre Fußsohlen mit dem ulkigen ‚Thermaltanz' und hebt die Füße abwechselnd vom glühenden Sand hoch.

SPECTACULAR NAMIBIA

sossusvlei

SOSSUSVLEI AFTER THE FLOODS

Once in 10 years torrential rains send the Tsauchab River down the Naukluft's canyons in flood, filling the main vlei at Sossusvlei (ABOVE) overnight. The river quickly subsides, but the water remains in the vlei, attracting waterbirds and insects. Flowering plants soon abound – waterlilies and yellow devil's thorn flowers carpet the water's edge, and the surrounding countryside is transformed (OPPOSITE). Here the annual rainfall may be less than 60 millimetres and evaporation exceeds precipitation by 200 times. But, when it does rain, the plants absorb the moisture greedily, providing enough liquid nourishment to sustain the world's largest population of dune creatures.

TRANSFORMED BY RAIN

Alle zehn Jahre führen heftige Regengüsse dazu, daß die Flutmassen des Tsauchab durch die Schluchten der Naukluft fließen und die große Senke am Sossusvlei (UMSEITIG) übernacht mit Wasser füllen. Der Fluß fließt schnell ab, aber das Wasser in der Senke bleibt und lockt Wasservögel und Insekten an. Bald steht alles in Blüte – Wasserlilien und gelbe Morgensternblumen bedecken die Ufer, und die umliegende Landschaft ist nicht wieder zu erkennen (OBEN). Die Niederschlagsmenge liegt hier unter 60 Millimeter, und die Verdunstung überschreitet sie um das 200fache. Aber, wenn es regnet, saugen die Pflanzen die Feuchtigkeit auf und versorgen die welthöchste Anzahl Lebewesen in Dünen.

THE SANDS OF SOSSUSVLEI

HOT-AIR BALLOONING

Sculpted by the wind over millions of years, the dunescapes of Namibia extend for several hundred kilometres, from the Gariep River in the south to Swakopmund in the north, and beyond. But nowhere are they more beautiful than at Sossusvlei (OPPOSITE) towards the southern end of the Namib-Naukluft Park. Soaring to heights of more than 350 metres, these dunes are the tallest in the world. Visitors to the nearby NamibRand Nature Reserve can view the panorama of Sossusvlei's dune seas from a hot-air balloon (RIGHT).

Die Dünenlandschaft der Namib wurde über Jahrmillionen vom Wind gebildet und erstreckt sich über etliche hundert Kilometer, vom Gariepfluß im Süden bis nach Swakopmund und noch weiter nördlich hinauf. Doch nirgendwo ist sie prächtiger als im südlichen Teil des Namib-Naukluft-Parks am Sossusvlei (UMSEITIG). Einige Dünen sind mehr als 350 Meter hoch – die höchsten Dünen der Welt. Besucher im nahe gelegenen NamibRand-Naturschutzgebiet können das Dünenmeer vom Heißluftballon aus genießen (RECHTS).

SPECTACULAR NAMIBIA

sossusvlei

DEAD PAN

The apricot and ochre tints of the dunes at Sossusvlei contrast sharply with the dazzling white surfaces of the clay pans. At the foot of Sossusvlei's highest dune lies Dead Pan (ABOVE), whose cracked surface is punctuated by mounds of sand which have collected around nara bushes. Dry as dust, achingly hot, the pan seems as if it has never seen rain. The little rain that does fall disappears within seconds. There is an ageless beauty about Dead Pan, whose scarred surface reflects the work of the sun and wind over millions of years. These same multi-directional winds have created sinuous lines and symmetrical sculptures in the sand between the dunes at Sossusvlei (OPPOSITE).

WIND-RIPPLED SAND

Die aprikosen- und ockerfarbenen Schattierungen der Dünen am Sossusvlei bilden einen starken Kontrast zu der weißlichen Schicht auf den Lehmpfannen. Am Fuße der höchsten Düne am Sossusvlei liegt die Tote Pfanne (UMSEITIG), deren rissige Oberfläche von Sandhügelchen, die sich um Narabüsche angesammelt haben, unterbrochen wird. Die Pfanne wirkt staubtrocken und erdrückend heiß. Das bißchen Regen, das fällt, versickert binnen Sekunden. Die zeitlose Schönheit der Toten Pfanne mit ihrer schorfigen Oberfläche ist das Werk von Sonne und Winden, die auch die geschmeidigen Linien und symmetrischen Sandskulpturen der Dünen bei Sossusvlei bewirken (OBEN).

SPECTACULAR NAMIBIA

sossusvlei

CAMEL THORNS, SOSSUSVLEI

The life-giving waters of the Tsauchab River provide enough sub-surface moisture to sustain camel thorn trees and a scattering of small plants and grasses in the main vlei at the base of Sossusvlei's dunes (ABOVE). While sub-surface water reaches this last oasis in the southern Namib Desert, it does not get as far as Dead Pan (OPPOSITE). Here the skeletons of camel thorn trees stand in a waterless wasteland. These trees have been dead for more than 500 years, their ancient trunks and branches preserved by the dry air and the lack of elements required to decompose them. The pans and the dunes which surround them have become one of Namibia's premier tourist attractions.

ANCIENT TREES, DEAD PAN

Tief unter der Erdoberfläche ermöglicht das Wasser des Tsauchabflusses das Überleben der Kameldornbäume und kleiner Pflanzen und Gräser in der Senke am Fuße der Dünen um den Sossusvlei (UMSEITIG). Das unterirdische Wasser erreicht noch diese letzte Oase in der südlichen Namibwüste, aber bis zur Toten Pfanne (OBEN) gelangt es nicht. Hier stehen die Gerippe der Kameldornbäume, die vor mehr als 500 Jahren abgestorben sind, in gänzlich ausgetrockneter Öde. Stämme und Äste sind konserviert durch die trockene Luft und Abwesenheit von abbaufähigen Elementen. Mit den umliegenden Pfannen und Dünen zählen sie zu den größten Touristenattraktionen in Namibia.

SPECTACULAR NAMIBIA

sossusvlei

WILDERNESS CAMP

Perched on a mountain overlooking the dunes is the Sossusvlei Wilderness Camp (ABOVE), which lies in a 19,000-hectare reserve with striking desert scenery. The camp is just 20 kilometres from Sesriem, and its brick, rock, timber and thatch units blend into the natural mountain environment. The reserve is home to a variety of wildlife, including gemsbok, springbok, bat-eared fox, Cape fox, brown hyaena and aardvark. On offer are ballooning safaris with spectacular views of the desert, as well as picnics under the camel thorn trees at Sossusvlei. Another popular attraction is the Sossusvlei Karos Lodge (OPPOSITE), which offers adobe-style units and luxury tents on the edge of the southern Namib's grasslands.

KAROS LODGE

Das Sossusvlei Wilderness Camp (UMSEITIG) liegt auf einem Berg in einem 19 000 Hektar großen Naturschutzgebiet und bietet einen herrlichen Ausblick über die Wüste. Nur 20 Kilometer von Sesriem entfernt, fügt sich das Rastlager mit Einheiten aus Ziegeln, Naturstein und Strohdach harmonisch in die Berglandschaft. Es gibt viel Wild, wie Oryxantilopen, Springböcke, Löffelhunde, Kapfüchse, braune Hyänen und Erdferkel. Safaris im Heißluftballon bieten eine atemberaubende Perspektive der Wüste. Ebenfalls beliebt ist die Sossusvlei Karos Lodge (OBEN), wo es Unterkünfte aus ungebrannten Lehmziegeln und Luxuszelte am südlichen Rand der schütteren Grasflächen gibt.

SPECTACULAR NAMIBIA

sesriem

DUNE ELIM

The silken sands of Dune Elim (ABOVE) provide a breathtaking view across the plains of southern Namibia, towards the Naukluft Mountains in the east (ABOVE and OPPOSITE) and the sand dunes in the west. Dune Elim flanks the dusty road to Sossusvlei, about five kilometres from Sesriem, and, together with Dune 45, is one of the most photographed of the dunes near Sossusvlei. It takes about an hour to climb Dune Elim, which is so large it is sometimes mistaken for a mountain. The further from the coast the Namib's dunes are, the deeper their reddish-brown shades, as the sand of inland dunes has been exposed to coloration by iron oxides for longer than the lighter grains nearer the sea.

NAUKLUFT MOUNTAINS

Von dem seidenweichen Sand der Elim-Düne (UMSEITIG) hat man einen atemberaubenden Blick über die Flächen des südlichen Namibia, die sich im Osten bis zum Naukluftgebirge (UMSEITIG und RECHTS) und im Westen bis zum Dünenmeer erstrecken. Die Elim-Düne liegt an der staubigen Landstraße nach Sossusvlei, etwa 5 Kilometer von Sesriem entfernt, und gehört – wie auch Düne 45 – zu den meist fotografierten Dünen am Sossusvlei. Es dauert etwa eine Stunde, diese Düne, die mitunter für einen Berg gehalten wird, zu besteigen. Je weiter man ins Inland vordringt, desto kräftiger wird die rötlich-braune Schattierung der Namib-dünen, denn die Sandkörner hier sind schon viel länger der Einfärbung durch Eisenoxid ausgesetzt als die helleren Körnchen in Küstennähe.

sesriem

SESRIEM CANYON

SESRIEM FROM THE AIR

Over millions of years the Tsauchab River has worn the pavement of sandstone down, creating the Sesriem Canyon (OPPOSITE), a gorge 30 metres deep. From the air (ABOVE) the canyon appears as a ragged artery winding through the desert. Early settlers called the canyon Sesriem, because they drew water from it by lowering a bucket attached to six (*ses* in Afrikaans) lengths of hide rope (*rieme*).

Über Jahrmillionen hinweg hat der Tsauchab die Sandsteinflächen abgetragen, und so entstand der Sesriemcañon (UMSEITIG), eine 30 Meter tiefe Schlucht. Aus der Luft (OBEN) wirkt der Cañon wie eine zerklüftete Ader, die sich durch die Wüste windet. Die Siedler der Frühzeit nannten den Cañon ‚Sesriem', denn um Wasser heraufzuziehen, mußten sie den Eimer an sechs Riemenlängen herunterlassen.

SPECTACULAR NAMIBIA

sesriem

SESRIEM GRASSLANDS

Bounded by the brooding Naukluft Mountains are the grasslands around Sesriem (ABOVE), one of the most beautiful landscapes of Namibia. Here and there, among flowering camel thorns, are the burnt skeletons of long-dead trees, their branches forming ghostly silhouettes against the rocky horizons and endless blue skies (OPPOSITE). These grasslands are the domain of ground squirrel and mongoose, gemsbok and bat-eared fox, which thrive on the huge populations of subterranean insects. More than 200 species of beetle, 160 species of spider and several dozen species of desert ant provide nourishment for the insectivores of the grasslands.

CAMEL THORN SKELETONS

Die Grasebenen beim Sesriem (UMSEITIG), begrenzt von den düsteren Naukluftbergen, gehören zu den schönsten Landstrichen Namibias. Zwischen blühenden Kameldornbäumen ragen vereinzelt die verbrannten Gerippe abgestorbener Bäume auf; ihre Äste bilden gespenstische Silhouetten gegen den felsigen Hintergrund und das endlose Blau des Himmels (OBEN). Diese Grasebenen sind die Heimat von Erdhörnchen und Mangusten, Oryxantilopen und Löffelhunden. Die meisten ernähren sich von den vielen Insekten unter der Erde. Mehr als 200 Käferarten, 160 Spinnenarten und Dutzende Arten von Wüstenameisen bilden eine Speisekammer für die Insektenfresser der Grasebenen.

SPECTACULAR NAMIBIA

namib-naukluft park

NAMIB-NAUKLUFT VISTA

The dunes, plains and grasslands of the Namib-Naukluft Park are home to more creatures than any other desert in the world. In this park, Namibia's largest and the fourth largest conservation area on earth, the wind-borne mists which roll in from the sea every second day enable a variety of plants, grasses and trees (LEFT) to survive under scorching conditions. This flora, in turn, supplies nourishment to the animals of the desert. Moisture absorbed from the desert grasses by large mammals, such as these gemsbok (OPPOSITE), allows them to survive for months without drinking water. In times of severe drought gemsbok and other smaller mammals head for the fossil riverbeds to dig for tsamma melons and nara plants, both great sources of water.

GEMSBOK HERD

Die Dünen, Ebenen und Grasflächen des Namib-Naukluft-Park beheimaten mehr Lebewesen als irgend eine andere Wüste der Welt. Hier, in Namibias größtem Naturschutzgebiet, treibt der Wind die Nebelschwaden von der Küste ins Inland und ermöglicht Pflanzen, Gräsern und Bäumen (UMSEITIG) unter heißen und trockenen Bedingungen zu überleben. Sie bedeuten Nahrung für die Wüstentiere. Selbst große Säugetiere, wie Oryxantilopen (OBEN), nehmen durch das Wüstengras genügend Feuchtigkeit auf, um monatelang ohne Trinkwasser auszukommen. In extremen Trockenzeiten ziehen die Tiere in die steinigen Flußbetten und fressen Tsammamelonen oder Narapflanzen.

HIKING THE OLIVE TRAIL

The name Naukluft means 'narrow ravine' and there is no shortage of these in the Namib-Naukluft Park. Over the millennia, rainwater has cut into the dolomites, shale and limestone, dissolving the rock and forming steep kloofs, or gorges (OPPOSITE). In the valleys below these rock walls, crystal-clear springs and pools rise from the ground, providing water and cooling dips for animals and humans. These pools are adorned with attractive formations of smooth tufa, limestone that has been re-deposited by the water over waterfalls. The 10-kilometre Olive Trail (ABOVE) and the Waterkloof Trail are day hikes which reveal the beauty of this enigmatic park, one of the most desolate in the world.

CLIMBING A DEEP RAVINE

Wie der Name schon sagt, herrscht in der Naukluft kein Mangel an engen Schluchten. Regenwasser hat sich über Jahrtausende durch Dolomit-, Schiefer- und Kalkgestein gefressen und tiefe Schluchten gebildet (RECHTS). In den Tälern unterhalb dieser Felswände entspringen kristallklare Quellen und bilden Wassertümpel – Labsal für Mensch und Tier. Zierliche Formationen von glattem Sinter, Kalkgestein, das sich oberhalb von Wasserfällen ablagert, haben sich um diese Wasserlöcher gebildet. Auf Wanderwegen, wie dem 10 Kilometer langen Olive Trail (UMSEITIG) und dem Waterkloof Trail kann man in Tageswanderungen die Schönheit dieses beeindruckenden Wildparks, einer der abgelegensten der Welt, erleben.

SPECTACULAR NAMIBIA

sandwich harbour

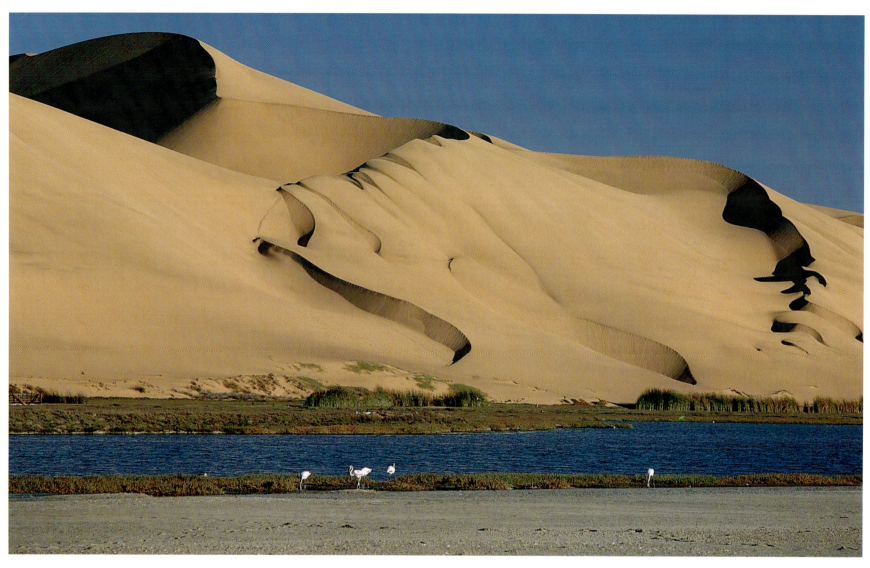

SAND DUNES ABOVE THE LAGOON

Ivory dunes tower above the reed-fringed lagoon at Sandwich Harbour (ABOVE), one of Namibia's most spectacular coastal destinations. Once known as Sandfisch Haven, the lagoon used to be open to the sea, but over the years it has silted up and is now a tranquil oasis for a variety of birds, including pelican and flamingo (OPPOSITE), as well as Hartlaub's gull. It is also an important breeding ground for several fish species. There is a certain mystique to Sandwich Harbour, fuelled by rumours that buried somewhere in the dunes is an old galleon filled with ivory, gold and precious stones. Sandwich, which lies 48 kilometres north of Walvis Bay, is popular with bird and nature lovers, and anglers, who record excellent catches.

LAGOON WATERBIRDS

Am Rande der mit Schilf umsäumten Lagune bei Sandwich Harbour türmen sich elfenbeinfarbene Dünen auf (UMSEITIG). Dies ist einer der schönsten Flecken an der Küste Namibias. Früher hatte die Lagune – einst bekannt als Sandfisch-Hafen – eine Öffnung zum Meer, die jedoch über die Jahre versandete. Jetzt ist es eine friedliche Oase für eine große Anzahl von Vögeln, einschließlich Pelikanen, Möwen und Flamingos (RECHTS). Außerdem laichen dort verschiedene Fischarten. Sandwich Harbour hat etwas Geheimnisvolles an sich, und dieses Gefühl wird verstärkt durch die Legende, daß irgendwo in den Dünen eine alte Galeere – beladen mit Elfenbein, Gold und Edelsteinen – vergraben liegt. Sandwich Harbour ist nur 48 Kilometer von Walvis Bay entfernt und sehr beliebt bei Naturliebhabern, Vogelbeobachtern und Anglern.

SPECTACULAR NAMIBIA

walvis bay

FISHING TRAWLER

The nutrient-rich waters of the Atlantic Ocean yield a good harvest of fish, providing a living for hundreds of Walvis Bay fishermen (ABOVE), who operate their trawlers in some of the world's most dangerous seas. Fish resources off the Namibian coastline, particularly anchovies and sardines, have been seriously depleted in recent years through over-exploitation by Spanish, Russian and Taiwanese trawlers. But Namibian authorities have now imposed strict controls and the fish populations are recovering, ensuring a reasonable livelihood for trawler crews. This mother and child (OPPOSITE) are part of the Topnaar group who live in the desert, some 30 kilometres outside Walvis Bay.

TOPNAAR WOMAN AND HER CHILD

Mutter und Kind (OBEN) gehören zu den Topnaars, die außerhalb von Walvis Bay in der Wüste leben. Die nährstoffreichen Gewässer des Atlantik liefern gute Fischzüge und sind die Grundlage für den Lebensunterhalt von hunderten von Fischern aus Walvis Bay (UMSEITIG), die ihre Kutter durch gefährliche Gewässer manövrieren müssen. Die Fischgründe entlang der namibischen Küste wurden in den letzten Jahren drastisch dezimiert als Folge von Überfischen durch große Fabrikschiffe aus Spanien, Rußland und Taiwan. Aber die namibischen Behörden haben jetzt strenge Kontrollen eingeführt, und die Fischgründe erholen sich und bieten wieder ein Auskommen für die Fischer auf den Kuttern.

SPECTACULAR NAMIBIA

swakopmund

82

SWAKOPMUND BEYOND THE DUNES

COASTAL GETAWAY

Namibia's favourite holiday resort, Swakopmund (OPPOSITE and ABOVE), resembles a small Bavarian village. Founded in 1892 by Captain Curt von François as the main harbour of German South West Africa (as Namibia was then known), its colonial character has been well preserved in its beautiful architecture. There is an old-world charm here that invites visitors to laze on sunny beaches or relax in one of the town's many restaurants.

Der beliebteste Erholungsort Namibias ist Swakopmund (UMSEITIG und OBEN). Der Ort, 1892 durch Hauptmann Curt von François als wichtigster Hafen für Deutsch-Südwestafrika gegründet, hat durch den Erhalt alter Bauwerke viel von seinem kolonialen Charakter behalten. Der Charme vergangener Zeiten lädt Besucher ein, sich am Strand in der Sonne zu aalen oder in einem der vielen Restaurants zu entspannen.

BAVARIAN ARCHITECTURE

The showpiece of Swakopmund, and perhaps the finest example of early Bavarian architecture in the town, is Woermann House (ABOVE). Designed by Friedrich Hoft and completed in 1905 as headquarters of the Damara and Namaqua Trading Company, it was fully restored in 1976. Its panelled walls and stucco ceilings have been admired by a host of local and foreign dignitaries, including Prince Albrecht of Prussia, who visited it in 1907. Other interesting examples of German architecture in Swakopmund are the Hohenzollern Building (OPPOSITE, TOP), which was built in 1906 as a hotel and now serves as a block of flats, and the Municipal Building (OPPOSITE, BOTTOM).

HISTORICAL BUILDINGS

Das architektonische Aushängeschild von Swakopmund ist das Woermannhaus (UMSEITIG), eines der schönsten Bauwerke im deutschen Kolonialstil. Der Entwurf stammt von Friedrich Hoft, und das 1905 vollendete Gebäude war der Hauptsitz der Damara- und Namaqua-Handelsgesellschaft. Es wurde 1976 vollständig restauriert. Die Fachwerkwände und Stuckdecken sind schon von vielen einheimischen und ausländichen Honoratioren bewundert worden, darunter Prinz Albrecht von Preußen, der 1907 den Ort besuchte. Weitere sehenswerte Beispiele deutscher Architektur in Swakopmund sind das Hohenzollern Haus (RECHTS, OBEN), das 1906 als Hotel gebaut wurde und jetzt Wohnungen enthält, und das Alte Amtsgericht, in dem jetzt die Stadtverwaltung untergebracht ist (RECHTS, UNTEN).

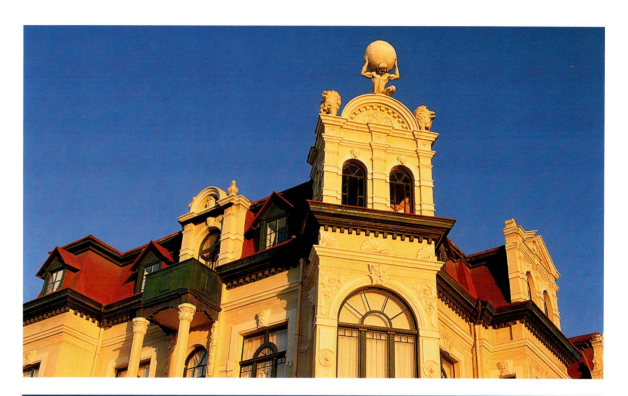

CAMEL RIDING NEAR SWAKOPMUND

Because of the freezing temperatures of the ocean and treacherous conditions offshore, residents of Swakopmund have had to turn to recreational pursuits other than swimming and boating. Among these are camel rides (ABOVE), and sandboarding and quad-bike riding (OPPOSITE) on the dunes between Swakopmund and Walvis Bay. Companies in Swakopmund offer full-day excursions to the dunes, with sandboarding tuition included in the price. Another option is hot-air ballooning over the desert and Rossing Mountain, with magnificent views of the Spitzkoppe, and the Naukluft ranges in the south. Parasailing trips to the dunes and mountaineering excursions to the Spitzkoppe are also available.

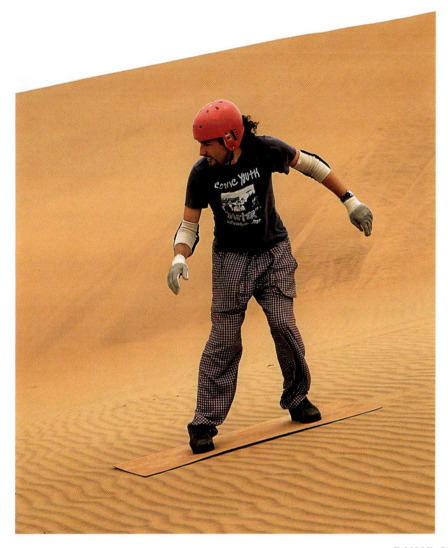 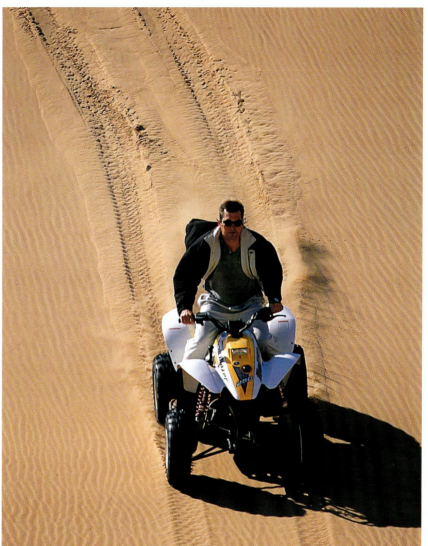

DUNE SPORTS

Das Meerwasser ist meistens kalt, und es gibt gefährliche Strömungen, also mußten sich die Swakopmunder außer Baden und Bootfahren auch andere Freizeitbeschäftigungen einfallen lassen. Dazu zählen Ausritte auf Kamelen (UMSEITIG) und sich auf Sandbrettern und Vierrädern (OBEN) in den Dünen zwischen Swakopmund und Walvis Bay zu vergnügen. Veranstalter in Swakopmund bieten Tagesausflüge an – Unterricht im Sandbrettfahren eingeschlossen. Man kann auch mit dem Heißluftballon aufsteigen und über die Wüste fliegen, wobei sich fantastische Ausblicke auf die Spitzkoppe und die Naukluftberge bieten, Gleitschirmfliegen in den Dünen oder Bergsteigen auf der Spitzkoppe.

CAPE CROSS SEAL RESERVE

The din of baying seals mixes with the sound of the crashing surf at the Cape Cross Seal Reserve (ABOVE), north of Swakopmund. This colony is the largest of Cape fur seals – during the November to December breeding season more than 150,000 can be seen on the rocks. The bulls are large, weighing up to 300 kilograms, but they are often too slow to protect their pups from marauding black-backed jackals and brown hyaenas who trot up and down along the beach. The Cape Cross Reserve, proclaimed in 1968, marks the spot where Portuguese navigator Diego Cão planted a stone cross in 1486. A replica can be viewed at the site where the original cross was erected (OPPOSITE).

CAPE CROSS

Das Bellen der Seehunde übertönt die Brandung bei der Robbenkolonie am Kreuzkap (UMSEITIG), nördlich von Swakopmund. Es ist die größte Kolonie von Kap Pelzrobben – während der Paarungszeit im November und Dezember halten sich mehr als 150 000 auf den Felsen auf. Die Bullen sind groß und wiegen bis zu 300 Kilogramm, aber sie sind oft zu schwerfällig, um ihre Jungen vor den räuberischen Schabrackenschakalen und braunen Hyänen zu schützen, die am Strand umherwandern. Das Schutzgebiet am Kreuzkap kennzeichnet die Stelle, wo der portugiesische Seefahrer Diego Cão 1486 eine Kreuzsäule errichtete. Jetzt steht eine Nachbildung an der Stelle (OBEN).

SPECTACULAR NAMIBIA

spitzkoppe

NATURAL ROCK ARCH

Wind, water and sand have created an extraordinary gallery of rock sculpture on Gross Spitzkoppe, an *Inselberg*, or mountain island, towering 1,728 metres over the plains west of Usakos. Among these forms is a natural arch, with bone-like seams of rock (ABOVE) and giant rounded boulders (OPPOSITE). To the southwest is the 1,572-metre Klein Spitzkoppe. The Gross Spitzkoppe, known as the 'Matterhorn of Africa', and this smaller formation are the skeletons of granitic lava which choked the cores of volcanoes created during seismic eruptions between 190 and 160 million years ago. Over the centuries these cores have been worn down to reveal their strange forms.

SPITZKOPPE BOULDERS

Wind, Wasser und Sand haben bei der Großen Spitzkoppe, einem *Inselberg,* der 1 728 Meter über den Ebenen westlich von Usakos aufragt, eine Galerie von Steinskulpturen geschaffen. Dazu zählen auch dieser Gesteinsbogen (UMSEITIG) und die riesigen Rundfelsen (OBEN). Die Große Spitzkoppe wird manchmal als ‚Matterhorn Afrikas' bezeichnet. Südwestlich davon liegt die 1 572 Meter hohe Kleine Spitzkoppe. Beide Bergmassive sind Reste von granitartigem Lavagestein, das die Vulkankrater, die während seismischer Eruptionen vor 190 bis 160 Millionen Jahren entstanden, verschloß. Über die Jahrhunderte wurden diese Krater abgetragen und ihre eigenartigen Formationen bloßgelegt.

SPECTACULAR NAMIBIA

spitzkoppe

92

THE SPITZKOPPE

Few sights in Namibia are more spectacular or more photographed than the slopes of the Spitzkoppe bathed in the light of the setting sun (ABOVE). The colours of these *Inselberge* are constantly changing, from apricot to fawn, orange to cerise, depending on the time of day and the position of the sun. Apart from their great scenic beauty the Spitzkoppe contain many precious stones and minerals. The western face of the Gross Spitzkoppe was first climbed in 1946 and since then the mountain has challenged the skills of mountaineers from around the world (OPPOSITE). For nature lovers there is a small campsite and the chance to take long walks and enjoy the abundant birdlife and clear starry skies.

CLIMBING THE SPITZKOPPE

Kaum ein Landschaftsbild in Namibia wird mehr fotografiert als der beeindruckende Anblick der Spitzkoppe im Licht der Abendsonne (UMSEITIG). Die Farbschattierungen dieser *Inselberge* verändern sich ständig, von aprikosen- bis rehfarben, von orange bis kirschrot, je nach Stand der Sonne oder Tageszeit. Abgesehen von dem schönen Anblick hat die Spitzkoppe auch Halbedelsteine und andere Mineralien aufzuweisen. Die Westseite der Großen Spitzkoppe wurde 1946 erstmalig erstiegen. Seitdem lockt der Berg Bergsteiger aus aller Welt (OBEN). Naturliebhaber finden einen kleinen Lagerplatz vor und genießen lange Wanderungen, das vielfältige Vogelleben und den klaren Sternenhimmel.

SPECTACULAR NAMIBIA

messum crater

WELWITSCHIA IN MESSUM CRATER

Like the skeletons of some prehistoric plant, the crumpled heaps of *Welwitschia mirabilis* (ABOVE and OPPOSITE, BOTTOM) lie scattered across the plains of the Messum Crater, southwest of the Brandberg Mountains. But these plants, among the most extraordinary in the world, are very much alive, and some, like the Great Welwitschia of the Huseb, are more than 1,500 years old. Charles Darwin called welwitschia the 'platypus of the plant kingdom'. In its lifetime, this botanical curiosity grows only two long leaves, which are shredded by the hot desert winds. The leaves and cones of the female plant provide nourishment for a variety of insects, including *Probergothis sexpunctatus* (OPPOSITE, TOP).

LIVING FOSSILS

Wie Gerippe aus prähistorischer Zeit liegen die verschlungenen Haufen der *Welwitschia mirabilis* (UMSEITIG und RECHTS, UNTEN) verstreut auf der Fläche des Messum-Kraters, südwestlich vom Brandberg. Aber diese einzigartigen Pflanzen sind sehr wohl am Leben. Einige von ihnen, wie die Große Welwitschia am Huseb, sind mehr als 1 500 Jahre alt. Charles Darwin nannte die Welwitschia ‚Schnabeltier des Pflanzenreiches'. Im Laufe ihrer langen Lebenszeit wachsen dieser botanischen Kuriosität nur zwei Blätter, die von den heißen Wüstenwinden zerzaust werden. Blätter und Zapfen der weiblichen Pflanze bieten vielfältigen Insekten Nahrung, darunter auch *Probergothis sexpunctatus* (RECHTS, OBEN).

SPECTACULAR NAMIBIA

twyfelfontein

GREAT ROCKS OF TWYFELFONTEIN

The walls, overhangs and caves of Twyfelfontein (ABOVE) are home to one of the world's greatest galleries of rock art. The more than 2,500 Stone Age rock carvings here, dating back 6,000 years, provide a priceless record of early life in Namibia. The site is internationally acclaimed, not only for the quantity, but also for the quality of the artwork. This mountainous region was named Twyfelfontein or 'doubtful fountain' by a farmer who was convinced a local spring would not provide enough water to support his cattle. Nearby are the Organ Pipes (OPPOSITE), a mass of perpendicular dolerite pillars in a riverbed. They were formed by the intrusion of volcanic dolerite 120 million years ago.

ORGAN PIPES

An den Felswänden und -überhängen der Höhlen bei Twyfelfontein (UMSEITIG) befindet sich eine der größten Galerien von Felsmalerei. Mehr als 2 500 Felsgravierungen aus der Steinzeit, einige mehr als 6 000 Jahre alt, bieten Aufzeichnungen über das Leben in Namibia in früheren Zeiten. Die Fundstätte ist international berühmt, sowohl für die Anzahl der Kunstwerke, als auch für die Qualität. Dieses bergige Gebiet nannte ein Farmer Twyfelfontein – ‚zweifelhafte Quelle' – da er befürchtete, daß die Quelle nicht ausreichend Wasser für sein Vieh spenden würde. In der Nähe sind die Orgelpfeifen (OBEN), senkrecht aufragende Doleritsäulen in einem Flußbett, gebildet vor 120 Millionen Jahren.

SPECTACULAR NAMIBIA

twyfelfontein

PREHISTORIC CARVINGS

Elephant, giraffe, antelope, rhino, lion and geometric forms are featured on the walls, overhangs and caves of Twyfelfontein. In common with most other prehistoric art sites in southern Africa, some of the depictions here of animal and human life are paintings (OPPOSITE), but what makes this site unusual are the many engravings or petroglyphs (ABOVE) that have been etched into the sandstone, dolomite or basaltic lava. A common theme is the representation of the tracks of certain animals. There is a lion on one of the rock galleries, with tracks affixed to its legs and etchings of forms half-human, half-animal. Some of the petroglyphs here have been worn down over the centuries and even defaced by graffitists.

ROCK ART

Elefanten, Giraffen, Antilopen, Nashörner, Löwen und geometrische Muster sind auf Felswänden und Überhängen in den Höhlen bei Twyfelfontein zu sehen. Diese Felskunst ist einmalig, da es sich – im Gegensatz zu den meisten prähistorischen Fundstätten im südlichen Afrika – nicht um Malereien (OBEN) sondern um Gravierungen oder Petroglyphen (UMSEITIG) handelt, die in Sandstein, Dolomit oder Lavabasalt eingeritzt wurden. Ein wiederholtes Motiv ist die Fußspur gewisser Tiere. In einer der Felsgalerien sieht man einen Löwen mit Spur und geritzte Gestalten, halb Mensch, halb Tier. Über die Jahrhunderte sind einige der Petroglyphen verwittert und andere mit Graffiti verunziert.

SPECTACULAR NAMIBIA

damaraland

GRASSLAND PLAIN

Open grasslands, rocky mountain ranges and dry riverbeds snaking towards the sea combine to make Damaraland a particularly beautiful area of Namibia (ABOVE). This part of the country is best known for the Brandberg Mountains with their San rock art and vistas of open plains and valleys. It is also the home of the Damara people (OPPOSITE), one of the oldest cultural groups in the country. Today, although many of the 105,000 Damara have migrated to the cities, those remaining in rural areas still successfully practise horticulture, concentrating on growing tobacco and pumpkins, although often relying on livestock as an alternative source of income.

RURAL TRANSPORT

Das Nebeneinander offener Grasflächen, felsiger Gebirge und trockener Flußbetten, die sich zur Küste winden, machen das Damaraland zu einem besonders malerischen Gebiet in Namibia (UMSEITIG). Bekannt ist dieser Landstrich für den Brandberg, mit Felsmalereien der San, und den weiten Ausblick über die offenen Flächen und Täler. Hier ist auch die Heimat der Damara (OBEN), eine der ältesten Volksgruppen des Landes. Obgleich viele der 105 000 Damara inzwischen in die Städte verzogen sind, betreiben die Verbliebenen erfolgreichen Pflanzenanbau, besonders Tabak und Kürbisse, aber Viehzucht bleibt eine wichtige zusätzliche Einkommensquelle.

SPECTACULAR NAMIBIA

damaraland

ENDANGERED BLACK RHINO

ROCK FORMS

Massive granite hills are a striking feature of the Damaraland terrain, which has become an important refuge for the endangered black rhino (OPPOSITE). By 1980 there were only 60 rhino in Damaraland as a result of indiscriminate poaching, but strict conservation has increased the number to 117 today. Bizarre Damaraland rockscapes such as these human-like forms (ABOVE) date back to between 130 and 150 million years.

Hügelige Granitmassive sind typisch für das Damaraland, ein wichtiges Schutzgebiet für das bedrohte Spitzmaulnashorn (UMSEITIG). Durch maßlose Wilderei gab es 1980 nur noch 60 Nashörner im Damaraland, aber strenge Schutzmaßnahmen haben die Anzahl bis auf 117 anwachsen lassen. Bizarre Felsformationen, wie diese menschenähnlichen Gebilde (OBEN) reichen 130 bis 150 Millionen Jahre zurück.

SPECTACULAR NAMIBIA

okonjati

MOUNT ETJO SAFARI LODGE

The manicured lawns and natural swimming pool of Mount Etjo Safari Lodge (ABOVE), 180 kilometres north of Windhoek, provide an ideal setting for guests looking for five-star treatment and superb game-viewing in the bush. Lying in the Okonjati Wildlife Sanctuary, the main lodge overlooks a waterhole where a variety of animals can be seen, including elephant, lion and hippo (OPPOSITE). The Mount Etjo (Etjo meaning 'place of refuge') area consists of 13,400 hectares of privately owned land and approximately 10,000 hectares of adjacent concessions. Apart from being the natural habitat of a number of large predators, it is also home to the diminutive Damara dik-dik, as well as giraffe and kudu.

ANIMALS OF OKONJATI

Mit gepflegten Rasenflächen und Schwimmbad bietet die Mount Etjo Safari Lodge (UMSEITIG), 180 Kilometer nördlich von Windhoek, ein ideales Umfeld für Gäste, die Fünf-Sterne-Komfort und ausgezeichnete Tierbeobachtung suchen. Die Lodge liegt im Okonjati Wildschutzgebiet, und das Hauptgebäude blickt auf eine Wasserstelle, wo viele verschiedene Tiere, einschließlich Elefanten, Löwen und Flußpferde (OBEN und RECHTS), beobachtet werden können. Das Areal von Mount Etjo (Etjo bedeutet Refugium) besteht aus 13 400 Hektar Land im Privatbesitz und etwa 10 000 Hektar angrenzender Konzessiongebiete. Abgesehen davon, daß es das natürliche Habitat einiger großer Raubtiere ist, beherbergt es auch den winzigen Damara Dik-Dik (Kleinantilope), sowie Giraffen und Kuduantilopen.

skeleton coast

DRY HUAB RIVERBED

The cracked clay surface of the frequently dry Huab River (ABOVE), in the southern reaches of the Skeleton Coast Park, reflects the constant – and often futile – battle of the elements to bring water to the sun-scorched desert. In times of good rain the river beats the high rate of evaporation, making it all the way to the sea. Over the millennia, the Huab has incised a valley through the sandstone pavement, creating a fertile linear oasis and lifeline for desert animals. Along the coast, the desolation of wind-swept shores is accentuated by mysterious circles of jagged stone (OPPOSITE), which, some surmise, could be the relics of ancient dwellings, although no-one is certain of their origins.

spectacular namibia

STONE CIRCLES

Die aufgeplatzte Lehmkruste in dem meist trockenen Flußlauf des Huab (UMSEITIG), an den südlichen Ausläufern des Skelettküsten-Parks, zeigt den ständigen – und oft vergeblichen – Kampf der Elemente, die sonnenverbrannte Wüste mit Wasser zu versorgen. Über Jahrmillionen hat der Huab, der in guten Regenzeiten trotz hoher Verdunstung bis zum Meer fließt, eine Talsenke durch den Sandstein gefurcht und bildet dadurch einen fruchtbaren Streifen für die Wüstentiere. An der Küste wird die Ödnis des windverwehten Strandes noch betont durch mysteriöse Kreise aus spitzen Steinen (OBEN) – von manchen als Überreste alter Behausungen angesehen, obwohl man nichts über den Ursprung weiß.

SPECTACULAR NAMIBIA

skeleton coast

108

WRECKED COASTER

The rusting hulks of dozens of ships, from small fishing boats and trawlers to passenger liners, lie half-buried in the sands of the Skeleton Coast. Also buried here are the bones of passengers and crew who, having survived the wreck, died of thirst on the waterless shore. Recently shipwrecked vessels, such as this coaster (ABOVE), are close to the high-water mark. But older wrecks, such as the *Eduard Bohlen* (OPPOSITE), which came to grief in 1909, lie 800 metres or more inland, engulfed by the sands of the Namib Desert. Early Portuguese mariners called the Skeleton Coast the 'Coast of Hell'. Reporter Sam Davis coined the name 'Skeleton Coast' in 1933, writing about a pilot missing on the Namibian coast.

WRECK OF THE EDUARD BOHLEN

Dutzende rostender Schiffsrümpfe, vom kleinen Fischkutter bis zum Passagierdampfer, liegen halb verschüttet im Sand an der Skelettküste. Ebenfalls hier begraben sind die Gebeine der Passagiere und Besatzungen, denn, auch wenn sie sich von dem Wrack retten konnten, sind sie an der wasserlosen Küste verdurstet. Unlängst aufgelaufene Schiffe, wie dieses Küstenschiff (UMSEITIG), liegen nah an der Flutlinie, aber alte Wracks, wie die 1909 gestrandete *Eduard Bohlen* (OBEN), liegen 800 und mehr Meter weit im Inland, von der Namibwüste verschluckt. Der Reporter Sam Davis erfand 1933 den Namen ‚Skelettküste' in seinem Bericht über einen an der Namibküste vermißten Piloten.

skeleton coast

110

NAFSI POROS WRECK

WEATHERED REMAINS

The half-buried Greek coaster, *Nafsi Poros* (OPPOSITE), wrecked in 1969, will soon be covered by the Namib Desert. In the meantime, the moist sea air rusts any exposed metal (RIGHT). The wrecks of the Skeleton Coast include the ships of 15th-century explorers, whose flimsy caravels, relying on the most rudimentary means of navigation, ran aground in the mists and strong currents. Other, more recent wrecks are the *South West Sea*, which floundered in 1976 near Toscanini, and the *Atlantic*, wrecked the following year at the mouth of the Uniab River.

Das halb verschüttete griechische Küstenschiff *Nafsi Poros* (UMSEITIG) ist 1969 gestrandet und wird bald mit Wüstensand bedeckt sein. Inzwischen rosten freistehende Metallteile in der Seeluft (RECHTS). Unter den Wracks an der Skelettküste sind auch Schiffe von Entdeckungsreisenden des 15. Jahrhunderts, deren unstabile Karavellen, auf notdürftige Navigationsmittel angewiesen, Nebel und starken Strömungen zum Opfer fielen. Eines der neuzeitlichen Schiffsunglücke ist die *South West Sea*, die 1976 bei Toscanini aufgelaufen ist.

CAPE FUR SEALS

Cape fur seals thrive on the Skeleton Coast (ABOVE) where the upwelling of the cold Benguela Current brings billions of nutrient-rich organisms to the surface, attracting vast shoals of pilchards, mackerel and anchovies. There are an estimated 750,000 to one million seals along the coast. Apart from predators, such as brown hyaenas and black-backed jackals (OPPOSITE) who prey on their pups, the seals' greatest threat is warm water. More than 200,000 (95 per cent) of the pups born in 1993 died the following year after fish deserted the unseasonably warm waters. Humans are another threat – every year about 25,000 pups are clubbed to death for their fur, an event which outrages animal rights groups.

BLACK-BACKED JACKAL

Kap-Pelzrobben gedeihen an der Skelettküste (UMSEITIG), wo die nährstoffreiche, kalte Benguelaströmung riesige Schwärme von Sardinen, Sardellen und Makrelen anlockt und 750 000 bis 1 Million Robben ernährt. Abgesehen von Raubtieren, wie braunen Hyänen und Schabrackenschakalen (OBEN), die sich an den Welpen vergreifen, besteht die größte Gefahr im Erwärmen des Meerwassers. Mehr als 200 000 (95 Prozent) der 1993 geborenen Jungen starben im darauffolgenden Jahr, weil die Fischschwärme durch unzeitgemäß wärmeres Seewasser ausblieben. Menschen sind die andere Bedrohung – alljährlich werden etwa 25 000 kleine Robben ihres Pelzes wegen totgeschlagen.

kaokoland

KUNENE RIVER

EPUPA FALLS

The Kunene River, forming Namibia's northern border with Angola, cuts through Kaokoland (OPPOSITE) before reaching the Ruacana and then the Epupa Falls (ABOVE). *Epupa* is Herero for 'spray' – referring to the spume of the cascades, which drop 60 metres. The campsite at Epupa Falls, with its palms, wild figs and baobabs, attracts birds such as the rufous-tailed palm thrush, bee-eaters, African fish eagles and malachite kingfishers.

Der Kunenefluß, Namibias nördliche Grenze mit Angola, schneidet durch das Kaokoland (UMSEITIG) ehe er erst die Ruacana- und dann die Epupa-Fälle erreicht (OBEN). *Epupa* bedeutet in der Hererosprache ‚Sprühen'. Der Lagerplatz bei den Epupa-Fällen, wo Palmen, Affenbrotbäume und wilde Feigenbäume stehen, lockt viele Vögel, wie rotschwänzige Palmdrosseln, Bienenfresser, Eisvögel und Schreiseeadler an.

SPECTACULAR NAMIBIA

kaokoland

RAFTERS MEETING A HIMBA FAMILY

A party of river-rafters pauses on the Kunene to talk to a Himba family (ABOVE). These waters, formerly out of bounds during the bush war, have become a mecca for river-rafters and canoeists in recent years. Options range from casual day trips along peaceful stretches of the river, to riding rapids such as Birthday Chute (OPPOSITE). The most popular stretch is the 120-kilometre section between Ruacana and Epupa Falls. At Epupa Falls the river fans out into a series of channels before tumbling into a deep gorge. Between the two falls are the Zebra Mountains and a lively section of the river known as the 13 Rapids, the most daunting rapid being Ondruso Gorge, five kilometres from the start.

RIDING THE BIRTHDAY CHUTE RAPID

Floßfahrer unterbrechen ihre Fahrt auf dem Kunene, um mit einer Himba-Familie zu plaudern (UMSEITIG). Die Gewässer, die zur Zeit des Buschkrieges gesperrt waren, sind in den letzten Jahren ein wahres Mekka für Floß- und Kanufahrer geworden. Man hat die Wahl zwischen den ruhigen Zonen des Flusses oder den Stromschnellen, wie die Birthday Chute (OBEN). Am beliebtesten ist die 120 Kilometer lange Strecke zwischen den Ruacana- und den Epupa-Fällen. Bei den Epupa-Fällen teilt sich der Fluß in mehrere Arme, ehe er die tiefe Schlucht hinabstürzt. Zwischen beiden Wasserfällen liegen die Zebra-Berge und eine turbulente Flußstrecke, bekannt als ‚die 13 Stromschnellen'.

SPECTACULAR NAMIBIA

kaokoland

118

LUSH KAOKOLAND VALLEY

Rugged, cone-shaped mountains dominate the skyline in Kaokoland (ABOVE), one of the last true wildernesses of southern Africa. In spite of soaring summer temperatures and a perennial lack of water, good downpours bring out thousands of flowers, like those of the puncture vine or caltrop plant (OPPOSITE), which burst into bloom in the company of wild fig, mopane and baobab trees. Seasonal rains bring much-needed relief to the dry riverbeds, whose vegetation nourishes the desert elephants, rhino and giraffe of the region. Kaokoveld's landscapes are particularly beautiful in the early morning and evening, when the mountains reflect the rising or setting sun.

CALTROP FLOWERS

Im Kaokoland wird der Hintergrund von zerklüfteten, konischen Bergen beherrscht (UMSEITIG). Dies ist eines der letzten wahren Wildnisgebiete im südlichen Afrika. Ungeachtet sehr hoher Sommertemperaturen und anhaltendem Wassermangel, zaubern gute Regengüsse einen Blütenteppich, wie diesen aus Bürzeldorn unter den Mopane-, Affenbrot- und Wildfeigenbäumen (OBEN). In der Regenzeit kommt dringend benötigte Feuchtigkeit in die trockenen Flußbetten, deren Vegetation die dort lebenden Wüstenelefanten, Nashörner und Giraffen ernährt. Von besonderer Schönheit ist die Landschaft früh am Morgen oder Abend, wenn die auf- oder untergehende Sonne von den Bergen reflektiert wird.

SPECTACULAR NAMIBIA

kaokoland

CROSSING THE MARIENFLUSS VALLEY

A dusty track crosses the Marienfluss Valley (ABOVE) in Kaokoland, flanked by the Otjihipa Mountains in the east and the Hartmann Mountains in the west. To the south, a group of desert elephants, dwarfed by the magnitude of the surrounding countryside, crosses the fossil bed of the Hoarusib River near Purros (OPPOSITE). These elephants have adapted to survive in this harsh environment. During particularly dry periods they use their feet and trunks to dig deep holes in the sand to get to subterranean water, providing other animals with a chance to slake their thirst as well. While most African elephants drink daily, desert elephants can go without water for up to four days.

spectacular namibia

DESERT ELEPHANTS

Eine staubige Sandpiste führt durch das Tal des Marienflusses (UMSEITIG) im Kaokoland. Im Osten sind die Otjihipa-Berge und im Westen die Hartmann-Berge. Im Süden kreuzt eine Gruppe Wüstenelefanten, die in dieser Landschaft fast zwergenhaft wirken, das steinige Flußbett des Hoarusib bei Purros (OBEN). Diese Elefanten haben sich dem harschen Umfeld angepaßt. Während der ärgsten Trockenzeiten graben sie mit Füßen und Rüsseln tiefe Löcher in den Sand, um unterirdisches Wasser zu erreichen. Dadurch können auch andere Tiere ihren Durst löschen. Während andere afrikanische Elefanten täglich trinken, können Wüstenelefanten bis zu vier Tage ohne Wasser auskommen.

SPECTACULAR NAMIBIA

kaokoland

KAOKOLAND DUNES

An indigo sky forms a stunning backdrop to a contrasting landscape of sand and rock in the northwestern part of the Kaokoland region. This is one of the wildest parts of Namibia, only navigable by four-wheel-drive vehicle. A land of geological wonders, it is a photographer's dream, with fossil rivers winding through valleys of palm trees and baobabs towards the sea. Here the Himba people live in rustic villages – like the one near Sesfontein (OPPOSITE) – as they have for centuries. Sesfontein is the site of a charming rest camp called Fort Sesfontein, which has a swimming pool, restaurant, petrol pump and camping sites among a grove of palm trees.

HIMBA VILLAGE, SESFONTEIN

Der indigoblaue Himmel im Hintergrund bildet einen wunderbaren Kontrast zur Sand- und Felslandschaft im nordwestlichen Kaokoland (UMSEITIG). Dies ist eine der ungezähmtesten Gegenden von Namibia und nur von Fahrzeugen mit Allradantrieb zu befahren. Es ist ein Traumland für Fotografen, mit geologischen Wundern und versteinerten Flußläufen, die sich durch mit Palmen und Affenbrotbäumen bestandene Täler zur Küste winden. Hier leben die Himba in einfachen Siedlungen – wie diese bei Sesfontein (OBEN) – wie sie es seit Jahrhunderten getan haben. Das Rastlager dort heißt Fort Sesfontein und bietet Schwimmbad, Restaurant, Benzinpumpe und Zeltplätze im Palmenhain.

SPECTACULAR NAMIBIA

kaokoland

ETANGA KRAAL

Himba women relax outside their home at Etanga Kraal (ABOVE). Their houses are simple, cone-shaped dwellings constructed of saplings, bound together with palm leaves and plastered with mud and dung. The Himba are nomadic pastoralists who live off their goats and cattle. They wear adornments including iron and shell-beaded necklaces, wristbands, anklets and colourful belts and bracelets (OPPOSITE, LEFT). Young Himba girls are assigned various domestic duties, such as collecting wild plums, which they bring back home in baskets on their heads (OPPOSITE, RIGHT). Himba women are fond of intricate hairstyles and cosmetic applications of ochre dust mixed with butterfat.

YOUNG HIMBA GIRLS

Himbafrauen entspannen sich vor ihren Hütten im Etanga-Kral (UMSEITIG). Die Behausungen sind einfache, konische Konstruktionen aus Ästen, mit Palmblättern zusammengefügt und mit Lehm und Dung verputzt. Die Himba sind nomadische Viehzüchter, die von ihren Ziegen und Rindern leben. Sie tragen Schmuck, wie Halsreife aus Eisen mit Muscheln, Arm- und Fußreife und farbenfrohe Gürtel und Armbänder (OBEN, LINKS). Himbamädchen haben Pflichten, wie das Einsammeln wilder Pflaumen, die in Körben auf dem Kopf nach Hause getragen werden (OBEN, RECHTS). Himbafrauen legen großen Wert auf komplizierte Frisuren und reiben sich mit einer Mischung aus Butterfett und Ockerpulver ein.

SPECTACULAR NAMIBIA

etosha national park

FORT NAMUTONI

One of Africa's premier game sanctuaries, Etosha National Park in Namibia's far north is as popular for its rest camps as it is for its animals. Fort Namutoni (ABOVE), at the eastern entrance to the park, is a legacy of German colonial rule dating back to 1903. The fort was renovated in the early 1980s, and its rooms now provide tourist accommodation. Okaukuejo Rest Camp (OPPOSITE) lies at the park's southern entrance and has excellent facilities, including swimming pools and a restaurant. Okaukuejo, which means 'place of women', has a waterhole at the rest camp that attracts a huge variety of animals, including lions who come down to stalk prey at the water's edge.

OKAUKUEJO REST CAMP

Einer der besten Wildparks in ganz Afrika ist die Etoschapfanne im Norden Namibias, bekannt und beliebt für das Tierleben, aber auch für seine schönen Rastlager. Fort Namutoni (UMSEITIG), 1903 errichtet, liegt am Osteingang des Wildparks und ist ein Stück deutscher Kolonialgeschichte. Vor zwanzig Jahren wurde das Fort renoviert, und die Räumlichkeiten stehen jetzt Touristen zur Verfügung. Das Rastlager von Okaukuejo (RECHTS) liegt am Südeingang des Wildparks und bietet erstklassige Annehmlichkeiten, einschließlich Schwimmbad und Restaurant. Die Wasserstelle am Rastlager von Okaukuejo – ‚der Ort der Frauen' – lockt viele Tiere an, einschließlich Löwen, die in der Nähe des Wassers auf Beute lauern.

SPECTACULAR NAMIBIA

etosha national park

ZEBRA AND SPRINGBOK AT AN OKAUKUEJO WATERHOLE

In the summer rainy season of northern Namibia, tens of thousands of animals migrate from the Andoni Plains to the mopane woodlands, savannah thornveld and waterholes of Okaukuejo (ABOVE). Among the animals are at least 15 species of antelope, zebra, rhino, elephant and an array of predators, including lion, leopard and cheetah. Also to be seen are lappet-faced vultures, gemsbok and springbok (OPPOSITE), who revel in the abundance of water and vegetation. The Heikum San named this region Etosha, meaning 'place of dry water' – a reference to the huge pan that lies at the heart of the national park. The pan is the relic of a once-great lake which covered the region millions of years ago.

WATERHOLE VISITORS

Während der sommerlichen Regenzeit in Nord-Namibia ziehen Zehntausende von Tieren von den Andoni-Ebenen zu den Mopanewäldern, der Dornsavanne und den Wasserstellen von Okaukuejo (UMSEITIG). Darunter sind wenigstens 15 Antilopenarten, Zebras, Nashörner, Elefanten und verschiedene Raubtiere, wie Löwen, Leoparden und Geparden. Auch Ohrengeier, Oryxantilopen und Springböcke (OBEN und RECHTS) genießen das reichliche Wasser und den frischen Pflanzenwuchs. Die Heikum-San nannten dieses Gebiet Etoscha – ‚Ort des trockenen Wassers' – was sich auf die riesige Pfanne im Herzen des Nationalparks bezieht. Diese Pfanne ist ein Überbleibsel von einem großen See, der sich vor Millionen Jahren über die ganze Region erstreckte.

SPECTACULAR NAMIBIA

etosha national park

AFRICAN ELEPHANTS

LEOPARD NEAR HALALI REST CAMP

A family of African elephants trundles towards the waterhole at Okaukuejo Rest Camp (OPPOSITE). Etosha's 2,000 elephants are the tallest pachyderms in Africa, but have the smallest tusks because of a mineral deficiency in their diet. Large herds are made up of smaller family groups consisting of a matriarch, several adult cows and offspring of different ages. The park is also home to leopard, like this one yawning in the thorn veld (ABOVE).

Eine Elefantenfamilie pilgert zur Wasserstelle am Rastlager in Okaukuejo (UMSEITIG). Die 2 000 Elefanten der Etoschapfanne sind Afrikas größte Dickhäuter, aber sie haben die kleinsten Stoßzähne wegen mineralstoffarmer Nahrung. Große Herden bestehen aus kleineren Familiengruppen mit Leitkuh, anderen Kühen und Jungtieren. Auch Leoparden leben im Wildpark, wie dieser, der in der Dornsavanne so herzhaft gähnt (OBEN).

SPECTACULAR NAMIBIA

etosha national park

ETOSHA OSTRICHES

An adult ostrich and three juveniles prepare to take a drink at a waterhole in Etosha (ABOVE), while a trio of giraffes (OPPOSITE) approaches warily nearby. Waterholes are particularly dangerous places for most animals, as they are the preferred hunting ground of lions, who lie in wait behind bushes and trees. As most waterholes lie in a depression, escape from a charging lion means running uphill – an easy enough task for the fleet-footed ostrich, but difficult for giraffe, who have to splay their legs to lower their long necks and drink. The diet of Etosha lions ranges from small mammals to baby elephants, and a pride will not hesitate to tackle an adult giraffe, working together to bring it to the ground.

GIRAFFE AT A WATERHOLE

Ein ausgewachsener männlicher Strauß und drei Jungtiere wollen an einem Wasserloch in der Etoschapfanne trinken (UMSEITIG), während das Giraffentrio (RECHTS) sich bedachtsam nähert. Die meisten Tiere sind an Wasserstellen besonders gefährdet, denn es ist das bevorzugte Jagdgebiet für Löwen, die hinter Büschen und Bäumen auf der Lauer liegen. Da sich die meisten Wasserstellen in einer Senke befinden, führt der Fluchtweg vor einem angreifenden Löwen bergauf – kein Problem für den leichtfüßigen Strauß, aber schwierig für die Giraffe, die breitbeinig und mit ausgestrecktem Hals trinkt. Löwen in der Etoschapfanne reißen unterschiedliche Beutetiere, von kleinen Säugetieren bis zu Elefantenbabys, und eine Gruppe von Löwen greift durchaus eine Giraffe an und bringt sie gemeinsam zu Fall.

SPECTACULAR NAMIBIA

etosha national park

134

TENSE MOMENT NEAR THE WATERHOLE

A group of zebras warily eyes a lion as it pads past near a waterhole (ABOVE), but daytime is not a lion's preferred hunting time. Lion spend most of the day lazing in the shade of a mopane or acacia tree. Then, at night, sometimes under the light of the moon, they emerge from their resting places and set off in single file to hunt, often in co-operation with each other. Zebra are a major part of the diet of the 300 lions in Etosha, as are antelope such as springbok, impala and kudu. After a kill, lion will spend hours or even days at the same spot, until, sated, they wander off, leaving the remains of their kill to lappet-faced vultures (OPPOSITE), black-backed jackals and hyaenas.

LAPPET-FACED VULTURES

Eine Gruppe Zebras beobachtet argwöhnisch den Löwen, der an der Wasserstelle vorbeigeht (UMSEITIG). Aber Löwen jagen selten tagsüber, sondern verbringen die meiste Zeit damit, im Schatten eines Mopanebaumes oder einer Akazie zu faulenzen. Nachts, manchmal bei Mondlicht, erheben sie sich vom Lager um auf Jagd zu gehen und greifen oft gemeinsam an. Zebras bilden einen wichtigen Anteil der Ernährung der 300 Löwen, aber Antilopen, wie Springböcke, Impala und Kudu, gehören auch dazu. Nach dem Riß bleiben Löwen stunden- oder sogar tagelang an der Stelle, ehe sie gesättigt abziehen und die Reste den Ohrengeiern (OBEN), Schabrackenschakalen und Hyänen überlassen.

north central region

OWAMBO CATTLE HERDERS

Thunderclouds loom on the horizon as Owambo herders drive their cattle home in the north of Namibia (ABOVE), where the arid plains and rocky valleys of the south give way to lush grasslands scattered with palm trees. Formerly known as Ovamboland, this area now consists of the Omusati, Oshana, Ohangwena and Oshikoto regions. Owambo is the collective name for the eight groups who live here, many of them earning their living off cattle and goats. There are about 600,000 Owambos in Namibia, accounting for about 50 per cent of the population. Many of them, like the girls depicted (OPPOSITE), supplement their income by fishing with homemade nets.

OWAMBO GIRLS FISHING

Während sich im Hintergrund am Horizont Gewitterwolken bilden, treiben Owambohirten im Norden Namibias ihre Rinder heimwärts (UMSEITIG). Die trockenen Flächen und steinigen Täler des Südens gehen hier in fruchtbare Grassavanne mit Palmen über. Dieses Gebiet, das früher als Owamboland bekannt war, ist jetzt in die Regionen Omusati, Oshana, Ohangwena und Oshikoto eingeteilt. Owambo ist ein Sammelbegriff für die acht Gruppen, die hier leben und sich hauptsächlich von Viehzucht ernähren. In Namibia leben etwa 600 000 Owambos, ungefähr 50 Prozent der Bevölkerung. Fischfang mit handgearbeiteten Netzen (OBEN), nutzen viele zur Ergänzung des Einkommens.

waterberg plateau park

WATERBERG PLATEAU

SANDSTONE CLIFFS

Sandstone ramparts in the Waterberg Plateau Park (OPPOSITE and ABOVE) loom over thornbush plains. The park is home to endangered species such as black rhino, roan and sable antelope and tsessebe. Apart from over 200 bird species, and a rare breeding colony of Cape vultures, many predators, including cheetah, live here. The Waterberg is a relic of a larger elevated pavement of Etjo sandstone, worn away over 200 million years.

Felswände des Waterberg-Plateau-Parks (UMSEITIG und OBEN) ragen über die Dornsavanne hinaus. Der Wildpark beheimatet gefährdete Tierarten, wie Spitzmaulnashörner, Rappen-, Pferde- und Halbmondantilopen. Es gibt viele Raubtiere, einschließlich Geparden, und mehr als 200 Vogelarten. Der Waterberg ist Überbleibsel einer viel größeren Hochebene aus Etjo-Sandstein, die über 200 Millionen Jahre hinweg abgetragen wurde.

SPECTACULAR NAMIBIA

SAN VILLAGE, TSUMKWE

A cluster of thatch-and-pole homes (ABOVE) forms the heart of a San community in the Tsumkwe district of Namibia. Formerly known as Bushmanland, Tsumkwe, and an area to the west of it known as Nyae Nyae, are among the last refuges of the San, who, in Namibia, have dwindled to just 15,000 people. Fewer than 2,000 of the San follow the lifestyle of their ancestors, subsisting on the earth, hunting with poison-tipped arrows which they make themselves (OPPOSITE, LEFT) and wearing traditional adornments (OPPOSITE, RIGHT). Ravaged by colonisation, development and even the bullets of farmers, the San originally travelled, lived and hunted over large parts of southern Africa.

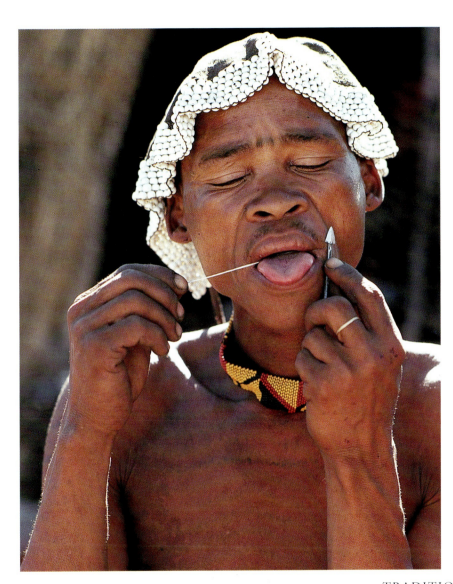 

TRADITIONAL SAN

Eine Gruppe strohgedeckter Hütten (UMSEITIG) bildet den Kern einer San-Gemeinschaft im Bezirk von Tsumkwe in Namibia. Früher nannte man das Gebiet Buschmannland, heute zählen Tsumkwe und das etwas weiter westlich gelegene Nyae Nyae zu den letzten Refugien der San, deren Bevölkerungszahl in Namibia auf 15 000 geschrumpft ist. Weniger als 2 000 San leben noch wie ihre Vorfahren von dem, was die Natur bietet, und was sie mit ihren selbstgefertigten Giftpfeilen erlegen können und tragen traditionellen Schmuck (OBEN). Ursprünglich zogen die San über weite Gebiete im südlichen Afrika, aber Kolonisation und moderne Entwicklung bereiteten ihrer Lebensweise ein Ende.

SPECTACULAR NAMIBIA

mudumu national park

142

PONTOON ON THE KWANDO RVIER

A pontoon from Lianshulu Lodge drifts lazily through the waters of the Kwando River in eastern Caprivi's Mudumu National Park (ABOVE), affording superb views of riverine birds and wildlife. There are more than 400 species of bird along Mudumu's waterways and in the surrounding bush, amongst them rufous-bellied heron, pygmy goose and western banded snake eagle. Hippos and crocodiles do not deter locals from commuting between riverbank villages by *mokoro* (OPPOSITE), a dugout canoe carved from the trunks of indigenous trees. Lianshulu Lodge is one of the finest in northern Namibia, offering game-drives in open four-wheel-drive vehicles and escorted trails through the bush on foot.

COMMUTING BY MOKORO

Ein Ponton (flaches Brückenboot) der Lianshulu Lodge dümpelt gemächlich auf dem Kwando-Fluss im Mudumu-Nationalpark in Ost-Caprivi (UMSEITIG) und bietet ausgezeichnete Beobachtungsmöglichkeiten von Vögeln und Tieren an den Flußufern. Mehr als 400 Vogelarten leben in Mudumu, darunter Rotbauchreiher, Afrikanische Zwerggänse und Bandschlangenadler. Flußpferde und Krokodile schrecken die Einwohner nicht davon ab, im Einbaum (*Mokoro*) zwischen den am Flußufer gelegenen Dörfern hin und her zu rudern (OBEN). Lianshulu Lodge, eines der schönsten Touristenlager in Nord-Namibia, bietet Pirschfahrten im Geländewagen und geführte Streifzüge durch den Busch.

SPECTACULAR NAMIBIA

kavango river

144

VILLAGERS ON THEIR WAY HOME

The lazy waters of the Kavango River (ABOVE) provide easy passage for the *mekoro* of two villagers heading home after a day's fishing. The Kavango forms a natural boundary between Namibia and Angola, and is Africa's only perennial river to flow east without reaching the ocean. After a journey of more than 1,000 kilometres, it spills out into the Okavango Delta floodplain, finally dying in the Kalahari's sands. The Kavango and its floodplains form the lifeline of the Kavango people, two thirds of whom live along the river's banks. Tending to their spiritual needs are Roman Catholic nuns (OPPOSITE, BOTTOM), who work at the Andara Mission (OPPOSITE, TOP), beside the Kavango.

ANDARA CATHOLIC MISSION

Die untergehende Sonne wird von dem träge dahinfließenden Kavango reflektiert (UMSEITIG), wo zwei Dorfbewohner nach den Fischzügen des Tages in ihren *Mekoro* heimwärts gleiten. Der Kavango bildet eine natürliche Grenze zwischen Namibia und Angola. Es ist der einzige immer fließende afrikanische Fluß, der ostwärts fließt, ohne den Ozean zu erreichen. Nach mehr als 1 000 Kilometern verteilt er sich über die Schwemmebenen des Okavango-Deltas und versickert schließlich im Sand der Kalahari. Der Kavango und seine Flutauen sind die Lebensgrundlage der Kavango, von denen Zwei Drittel an den Flußufern leben. Um ihr geistliches Wohl bemühen sich katholische Nonnen, die in der Missionsstation Andara am Kavango arbeiten (RECHTS).

kavango river

KAVANGO VILLAGE

A Kavango family tends to domestic chores, pounding maize and millet outside their home (OPPOSITE, TOP) near the Kavango River. Of the people living on the banks of the Kavango (ABOVE), about 140,000 earn their livelihood from animal husbandry, fishing (OPPOSITE, BOTTOM) and cultivating maize, some of which is used for local consumption. The Kavango people moved to the south of the Kavango River from Angola, between 1750 and 1800, and comprise five groups – the Kwangali, Mbunza, Shambyu, Gciriku and Mbukushu. Many have migrated to the cities to take up formal employment or sell handicrafts such as African masks, bowls, copper and bead accessories and furniture.

LIFE ON THE KAVANGO

Eine Kavangofamilie widmet sich ihren häuslichen Pflichten und stampft Mais und Hirse vor ihrer Hütte (RECHTS, OBEN) in der Nähe des Kavango. Von den Menschen, die an den Ufern des Kavango leben (UMSEITIG), verdienen sich etwa 140 000 ihren Lebensunterhalt durch Viehzucht, Fischfang (RECHTS, UNTEN) und Maisanbau. Ein Teil ist für eigenen Gebrauch bestimmt. Das Volk der Kavango ist zwischen 1750 und 1800 von Angola auf die Südseite des Kavango gezogen. Es gibt fünf Gruppen – die Kwangali, Mbunza, Shambyu, Gciriku und Mbukushu. Viele sind schon in die Städte gezogen, wo sie Arbeitsplätze fanden oder Handarbeiten wie afrikanische Masken, Gefäße, Möbelstücke, Kupfer- und Perlenschmuck an Touristen verkaufen.

SPECTACULAR NAMIBIA

zambezi river

FLOATING RIVER BAR

A floating river bar, silhouetted by the sun setting over the Zambezi River (ABOVE), provides a romantic venue for guests at the Zambezi River Lodge near Katima Mulilo. This part of the Zambezi, flanked by huge indigenous trees, is a birder's paradise, and trails organised by the lodge afford guests an excellent chance to see local wildlife. The Zambezi (OPPOSITE), which means 'great river', has its origin in western Zambia. It flows southwards to create one of the great natural wonders of the world, the Victoria Falls, on the border between Zimbabwe and Zambia, before continuing on to Mozambique. Teeming with crocodiles and hippos, it is popular for river-rafting and canoe trips.

THE ZAMBEZI AT SUNSET

Eine Flußbar, deren Umriß sich im Licht der untergehenden Sonne über dem Sambesi (UMSEITIG) abhebt, bildet einen romantischen Treffpunkt für Gäste der Sambesi River Lodge bei Katima Mulilo. Dieser Abschnitt des Sambesi, umgeben von einheimischen Bäumen, ist ein Paradies für Vogelbeobachter. Die Lodge bietet auch Streifzüge zur Wildbeobachtungen. Der Sambesi (OBEN) entspringt im Westen Sambias, fließt südwärts und bringt an der Grenze zwischen Sambia und Simbabwe eines der größten Naturwunder der Welt hervor, die Viktoria-Fälle, ehe er nach Mosambik weiterfließt. Trotz Krokodilen und Flußpferden ist der Fluß beliebt für Floß- und Kanufahrten.

SPECTACULAR NAMIBIA

kalembeza

CATTLE IN KALEMBEZA VILLAGE

A thatched *boma* serves as shelter from the heat of the Caprivi sun for these cattle in Kalembeza Village (ABOVE), while young herders set off from the village with their dogs and charges (OPPOSITE) to find grazing for the day. The Mafwe and the Masubia are the two main cultural groups in the Caprivi, a narrow piece of land that lies on Namibia's northeastern border with Angola, Botswana and Zambia. Most Caprivians are subsistence farmers, living off their own produce and fishing on the banks of the Zambezi, Kwando, Linyanti and Chobe rivers. Aside from this, villagers here do generate some income from cattle and goat farming. The cattle of this region are mostly Kashivi (formerly known as Nguni).

CAPRIVI HERDERS

Eine strohgedeckte *Boma* bietet diesen Rindern in der Kalembeza-Siedlung Schutz vor der gleißenden Sonne am Caprivi (UMSEITIG), während junge Hirten sich mit ihren Schutzbefohlenen und Hunden auf den Weg machen (OBEN), um Weide für den Tag zu finden. Das Volk der Caprivi bildet zwei Kulturgruppen, die Mafwe und die Masubia, die an der nordöstlichen Grenze Namibias mit Angola, Botswana und Sambia an den Flußufern des Caprivi leben. Die Mehrheit betreibt Subsistenzwirtschaft oder Fischerei an den Ufern der Flüsse Sambesi, Kwando, Linyanti und Chobe. Das Einkommen der Einwohner stammt überwiegend aus Rinder- und Ziegenzucht.

SPECTACULAR NAMIBIA

kwando river

152

KWANDO WATERLILIES

Waterlilies bring splashes of colour to the Kwando River which, in the rainy season, spills out into a floodplain 170 kilometres east of Popa Falls, providing lush pastures for the animals of the teak forests. Here, along the watercourses of the Kwando River, water-loving antelope, such as sitatunga, reedbuck, waterbuck and red lechwe, will be found grazing in the company of elephant, buffalo, Burchell's zebra and bushbuck.

Wasserlilien bringen Farbtupfer auf den Kwando, der sich zur Regenzeit über die Schwemmebenen, 170 Kilometer östlich der Popa-Fälle, ergießt und saftige grüne Weide für die Tiere der Teakwälder schafft. Hier, an den Wasserläufen des Kwando, weiden die Antilopen der Sumpfgebiete, wie Sitatunga, Großriedböcke, Ellipsen-Wasserböcke und Letschwe, zusammen mit Elefanten, Büffeln, Steppenzebras und Buschböcken.